The Ministry of Pensions and National Insurance

THE NEW WHITEHALL SERIES
is prepared under the auspices of
THE ROYAL INSTITUTE OF PUBLIC ADMINISTRATION
and is edited on its behalf by Sir Robert Fraser, O.B.E.
The purpose of the series is to provide
authoritative descriptions of the present work
of the major Departments of Central Government

Already published
THE HOME OFFICE (*reprinted*)
THE FOREIGN OFFICE (*reprinted*)
THE COLONIAL OFFICE
THE MINISTRY OF WORKS
THE SCOTTISH OFFICE
THE MINISTRY OF PENSIONS AND
NATIONAL INSURANCE

In Preparation
THE MINISTRY OF LABOUR AND
NATIONAL SERVICE
THE MINISTRY OF TRANSPORT
AND CIVIL AVIATION

THE NEW WHITEHALL SERIES

The Ministry of Pensions and National Insurance

SIR GEOFFREY S. KING

K.C.B., K.B.E., M.C.

Formerly Permanent Secretary to
the Ministry

LONDON . GEORGE ALLEN & UNWIN LTD
NEW YORK . OXFORD UNIVERSITY PRESS INC

FIRST PUBLISHED IN 1958

PRINTED IN GREAT BRITAIN
in 10 *point Times Roman type*
BY UNWIN BROTHERS LIMITED
WOKING AND LONDON

Foreword

★

THIS book describes how the Ministry of Pensions and National Insurance is organized, the work it does, the system of statutory authorities (the insurance officer, local tribunal and National Insurance Commissioner) who decide claims under the national insurance and industrial injuries schemes and the pensions appeal tribunals who hear appeals on claims to war pensions. It gives a general description of the various pensions benefits and allowances administered by the Ministry but it does not purport to be a complete guide to them. The early history of war pensions and the Ministry of Pensions is not dealt with but a short account of the earlier history of the other schemes is included in order to explain how they came to take their present shape.

I record my grateful thanks to former colleagues in the Ministry for many valuable suggestions and for pointing out a number of errors made in the course of preparing the text and especially to Miss G. M. Jones who also prepared the appendices for me. I must, however, make it clear that I alone am responsible for any comments or expressions of opinion the book may contain and that none of them are to be taken as in any way expressing official views.

G. S. KING

Contents

★

CHAPTER I

Introduction

*

THE Ministry of Pensions and National Insurance is concerned, almost exclusively, with the administration in Great Britain of four schemes that provide cash allowances designed to meet a wide variety of circumstances—war pensions, national insurance pensions and benefits, industrial injury benefits and family allowances, but it also carries out some agency services for other departments. War pensions are intended to compensate people who are injured in war or while serving in the armed forces of the Crown. The majority of war pensioners are in regular employment and they draw their pensions in addition to their wages. The national insurance scheme, which is the largest of the four schemes administered by the Ministry, provides a number of benefits for people when they are unable through sickness, unemployment or old age to earn their own living; it also provides maternity benefits and benefits for families that have lost their breadwinner. The main benefits are retirement pensions, widow's benefits and unemployment and sickness benefits. The industrial injury benefit scheme makes special provision for the man who is injured while at work or is suffering from an industrial disease. Family allowances are intended to help families with two or more children by providing a weekly allowance in respect of every child in a family after the first.

The existence of so many schemes, each with its own set of conditions which have to be satisfied before an allowance or pension can be paid, created a complex administrative problem that was made all the more complicated by the different financial arrangements for providing the money required to meet sums due to beneficiaries. War pensions and family allowances are paid out of moneys voted annually by Parliament. National insurance pensions and benefits are paid out of a special fund known as the National Insurance Fund, and there is a similar and separate fund for industrial injury benefits. These funds are under the control and management of the Minister of Pensions and National Insurance who is responsible for collecting the weekly insurance contributions, payable by some 24 million people insured under the national insurance schemes, which constitute the main source of income of the two funds.

9

The scale of the Ministry's operations can be illustrated by a few figures from the latest published accounts—those for 1956–7. The Ministry collects about £630 million a year in contributions. It pays out over £450 million a year in retirement pensions. Other national insurance benefits amount to about £200 million a year and industrial injury benefits to a further £35 million. War pensions account for about £90 million and family allowances for £114 million. In all, therefore, the Ministry collects over £600 million a year and pays out over £850 million at a cost in administrative expenses of about £45 million a year.

THE ORIGIN OF THE MINISTRY

The Ministry of Pensions and National Insurance came into existence in August, 1953, when the Ministry of Pensions (which until then had been responsible for the administration of war pensions) and the Ministry of National Insurance (which had been administering the other three schemes) were amalgamated. The Ministry of Pensions was established in 1916 to administer the scheme of war pensions introduced during the First World War and it also provided medical treatment and artificial limbs to disabled ex-service men. The Ministry of National Insurance was set up in 1944 in response to a general demand for a special Ministry to introduce and be responsible for the administration of new schemes of social security outlined in two White Papers presented to Parliament in 1944 by the war-time Coalition Government. By 1953 the work of the Ministry of Pensions was beginning to fall off, as it had done between the two wars; by then also the Ministry of National Insurance had successfully carried out its first task of launching the new schemes of social insurance and family allowances. The administration of war pensions had much in common with the benefit work of the Ministry of National Insurance and the medical side of the war pensions work could, it was felt, be more conveniently carried on as part of the National Health Service. It was therefore decided, in the interests of both economy and efficiency, to amalgamate the two Ministries and at the same time to transfer the medical functions of the Ministry of Pensions to the Ministry of Health. These steps were effected by means of Orders in Council under the Ministers of the Crown (Transfer of Functions) Act and the consequential administrative arrangements were carried through with surprisingly little difficulty.

OUTLINE OF THE MINISTRY'S ORGANIZATION

Although the Ministry collects and pays out huge sums every year it does not make large payments to individuals nor enter into large single contracts. It is concerned with a multiplicity of small payments and receipts and this is reflected in its organization, the key-note of which is decentralization wherever possible. Most of the men and women who claim benefits and pensions depend on what they get from the Ministry to meet their day-to-day expenses. They rely on the prompt and regular payment of sums due to them and any delay or interruption in the payments can cause serious hardship. Many of them, moreover, are ill or injured or too old to cope with complicated forms and procedures and must therefore be able to draw their money with the minimum of fuss and have help and advice available in case of difficulty. The day-to-day business of the Ministry has accordingly been brought as close to the public as possible and the local offices, of which there are about 900, are the basis of the Ministry's organization. To the member of the public with war pension or national insurance business on hand the local office is the Ministry, and every effort has been made to staff and equip these offices in such a way as to enable them to handle on the spot the public's business and queries. Pensioners and beneficiaries draw their pensions or benefits (other than unemployment benefit which continues to be administered and paid in cash through the Employment Exchange) by means of orders or postal drafts which can be cashed, as readily as postal orders, at one of the 25,000 or so Post Offices that handle national insurance business; facilities do exist for payment of benefits in cash at the Ministry's local offices but they are little used.

Behind the local office is an elaborate organization, of which the general public knows little, which carries out all the work that has to be done to ensure the prompt and accurate payment week by week of millions of pensions and benefits. This organization is responsible for the Parliamentary work of the Ministry; it deals with establishment questions arising out of the employment of a staff of over 36,000; it prepares and issues annually about 9 million pension and family allowance order books; it keeps the records of over 800,000 war pensioners, of over 24 million insured contributors and of $3\frac{1}{4}$ million families drawing family allowances; it provides local offices with much of the guidance and information they need to enable them to deal promptly with claims to pensions, benefits or allowances and generally guides and supervises their work.

This organization consists of three main parts.

There is the regional organization which, under the Controllers in Scotland and Wales and ten Regional Controllers in England, is responsible for the running of the local offices. The Central Offices are responsible for keeping the records and preparing and issuing order books for pensions. Most of this work is done at the office at

Long Benton near Newcastle upon Tyne, but war pensions records are kept, and indeed the bulk of the war pensions work is done, at Blackpool.

The headquarters of the Ministry, which has a comparatively small administrative staff under the Permanent Secretary, is in London. It is responsible for advising the Minister on all questions of policy affecting the work of the Department, whether they arise out of day-to-day work, are thrown up by the review of that work which is constantly going on, or are urged upon the Minister by Members of Parliament or by other bodies like the T.U.C. or the ex-service organizations specially interested in war pensions. It is also responsible for the co-ordination of the work of the Department with other Departments and especially with the Treasury, the Ministry of Health and the Ministry of Labour and National Service. It conducts the Parliamentary work of the Ministry including the preparation of answers to Parliamentary Questions and briefing of Ministers for debates. It is responsible for instructing Parliamentary Counsel in connection with Parliamentary Bills and for preparing regulations. This headquarters staff includes the Accountant-General, who is the head of the finance department of the Ministry; the Director of Establishments and Organization who is responsible for all matters affecting staff and organization; and the Under Secretaries each of whom is immediately responsible for one or more of the main schemes administered by the Department. There is also a medical branch which, under the Chief Medical Officer, deals with the organization and work of medical boards needed for war pension and industrial injury purposes and advises on medical matters affecting the work of the Ministry, and the legal department, under the Solicitor to the Ministry, which drafts regulations, advises on legal questions and conducts proceedings in the Courts for the prosecution of offences against the rules and regulations governing the payment of pensions and benefits, and for the enforcement of payment of contributions from defaulters, and also conducts proceedings in the High Court arising out of claims to war pensions or disputes about the insurable status of individuals.

Considerable use is made of central and local committees composed of members of the public, in connection with the work of the Ministry. The National Insurance Advisory Committee and the Industrial Injuries Advisory Council, both of which are central bodies based on London, in particular play an important part in the administration of the main national insurance and industrial injuries schemes. When regulations are needed under either of these schemes the Committee or the Council, as the case may be, is consulted while the proposals are still in draft and many changes in the original proposals have been made as the result of their advice. They have also carried out a number of important investigations into questions connected with the schemes, including some that have led to legislation. Some of these investigations have extended over long periods and their reports have always been of the greatest value in satisfying responsible opinion that the various problems which inevitably arise from time to time in connection with these huge schemes of national insurance are receiving thorough and independent consideration. The composition and functions of these and the other committees connected with the Ministry are described in detail in later chapters.

The main lines of the Ministry's organization have not been changed since they were originally laid down in 1946. Alteration in detail there has been; local offices have been closed here and opened there to meet the convenience of the public and the demands of the work, and changes have been made in forms and procedures in a continuous effort to smooth out difficulties thrown up in the course of administration. The review of the organization was hampered by the alterations in rates of contribution and benefit which have taken place in the years since the schemes were introduced in 1948. The main National Insurance Act contained elaborate provision for the quinquennial review of rates of benefit and contribution and it is a fair assumption that the original intention was that changes would not be made more frequently. In fact rates of pension were altered twice during the first quinquennial period and rates of other benefits and contributions once. All rates were altered again about a year after the second review period started and those now current were introduced early in 1958. Elaborate and complicated administrative arrangements are required to carry such changes into effect. They added considerably to the strain on the new administrative machine and while they were pending much other work had to be suspended to ensure that the changes were made smoothly and there was no interruption in the regular payment of pensions and benefits.

CHAPTER II

The Origins of the National Insurance and Allied Schemes

*

GENERAL

THE schemes administered by the Department have grown out of a long-felt desire for some way of providing for people who cannot earn their own living, either temporarily because of sickness or unemployment, or more permanently during widowhood or because of serious injury or old age, which did not entail what were regarded as the indignities of the Poor Law. It would be a mistake to imagine that these schemes were planned as a coherent whole; they have evolved gradually over the years and they embody what, at first sight, appears to be a curious mixture of administrative techniques.

The main national insurance scheme is contributory: weekly contributions have to be paid by the persons it covers and pensions and benefits are closely linked to the payment of those contributions; so that the claimant who has paid less than the full number of contributions due may find his pension or benefit reduced, and in certain circumstances it may be withheld altogether. The industrial injuries scheme is also contributory in so far as it involves the payment of weekly contributions, but the benefits payable under this scheme are not linked to the payment of contributions like benefits under the main scheme; they are payable in full even though the full number of contributions due has not been paid.

An important difference between the general scope of the two insurance schemes may be mentioned here. Under the main national insurance scheme a person is insured all the time regardless of what he is doing when something happens that may give rise to a claim to benefit; he will be entitled to sickness benefit, for example, whether he is at work or on holiday when he falls ill. Under the industrial injuries scheme, on the other hand, he is only covered while he is actually at work, and if he falls down and breaks a leg at home industrial injury benefit is not payable.

The war pensions scheme is part of the conditions of a man's service in the armed forces and has nothing to do with insurance; to be entitled to a war pension a man must have served in the forces and sustained a disability attributable to that service. Nor is the family allowance scheme based on insurance; there are no contributions for family allowances and the only qualification is the existence in a family of two or more children below the prescribed age.

There is no 'means test' attached to any of these schemes and in general a person who satisfies the conditions can draw his pension, benefit or allowance irrespective of any savings or personal income he may have. Widow's pensions and about a quarter of the retirement pensions are, however, subject to 'earnings rules' under which a pension will be reduced if the pensioner's earnings in any week exceed a specified amount; similar rules are used to determine whether a wife can be regarded as dependent on her husband for benefit purposes. These rules are really intended as tests of whether the conditions for the receipt of the pension or benefit are satisfied.

THE POOR LAW AND NATIONAL ASSISTANCE

The Poor Law and its history do not fall within the scope of this volume, but as the Minister of Pensions and National Insurance has certain responsibilities for National Assistance, which has taken the place of the Poor Law, a brief note of some salient points is desirable.

Some provision has always been made for people who could not support themselves, but it was not until the reign of Elizabeth I that it was systematized into something recognizable as the Poor Law of modern times. The Poor Law was a local service paid for out of local rates. It was originally based on the Parish but the administrative area was gradually widened until it became the County or County Borough with the Council as the Public Assistance (or Poor Law) Authority. This continued until 1931 when the Ministry of Labour, under what was known as the Transitional Payments Scheme, took over financial responsibility for the able-bodied unemployed who had exhausted their unemployment benefit; administrative responsibility remained with the Public Assistance Authority. This divorce of administrative from financial responsibility did not last long. In 1934 a central authority known as the Unemployment Assistance Board was set up and assumed financial and administrative responsibility for all able-bodied unemployed whose needs could not be met by unemployment insurance. The scope of the Board's functions was extended in 1941 to include the supplementation of old age pensions and its name was changed to 'Assistance Board'. In 1948 the Board took over from the Public Assistance Authorities what remained of their responsibility for outdoor or cash relief and became known by its present title of the 'National Assistance Board'.

For a long time the Poor Law was the only refuge of the destitute. It was based on the 'destitution test' under which an applicant was expected to exhaust his savings before getting relief; it also embodied the principle of 'liable relatives' under which certain relatives could be required to contribute towards an applicant's support. In administering the Poor Law, the 'household means test', under which account was taken of the means of all the members of the household of which the applicant for relief was a member, was also applied. The destitution test was gradually modified by the introduction of what are known as 'disregards'. These are rules which allow certain types of income to be ignored in deciding what relief to give. The list of disregards has been extended from time to time and in determining the amount of assistance to be granted quite a number of different types of resource are now disregarded. The doctrine of 'liable relatives' and the 'household means test' were abolished in 1943, and at present assistance is granted by the National Assistance Board on the basis of the resources of the applicant and his wife and no account is taken of the resources of other members of the household.

The Minister of Pensions and National Insurance is responsible for making the regulations under which assistance is paid but does so on the basis of a draft submitted to him by the National Assistance Board. He also answers in Parliament questions about the Board's work, his replies usually taking the form of passing on information supplied to him by the Board.

INDUSTRIAL INJURIES

The first step towards making provision for the destitute outside the Poor Law was taken in 1897 when the first Workmen's (Compensation for Accidents) Act, which made special provision for workmen injured while at work, was passed. Until then, an injured workman might have belonged to one of the benefit clubs which first became important forces in the lives of the workers during the early days of the Industrial Revolution, or he might have received help from some charitable source; usually, however, he had to resort to the Poor Law. In a few cases he might have been able to sue his employer for damages in the Courts but in order to succeed there he had to show that his injury was due to negligence on the part of the employer. This placed a heavy burden on him which in many cases he was unable to discharge; especially as his claim was liable to be defeated by a defence based on what was known as the 'doctrine of common employment' under which the employer might escape liability if he could show that the injury was due to the negligence of a fellow-workman; it being considered that the possibility of such injury must be regarded as a normal risk of employment.

The Workmen's Compensation Act of 1897 introduced a completely new principle. The workman no longer had to prove that his employer had been negligent; it was sufficient, in order to establish a claim to compensation, to show that he had been injured by an accident arising out of and in the course of his employment though his claim might in certain cases fail if the injury was shown to be due to his serious and wilful misconduct. Compensation usually took the form of a weekly payment equivalent (subject to an overriding maximum) to a proportion of his normal earnings, but sometimes a lump sum would be paid. Disputes were settled by a form of arbitration that differed little from proceedings in the Courts and, although something like 90 per cent of all claims to compensation were settled without resort to the Courts, the volume of litigation to which the scheme gave rise caused it to be viewed with disfavour in some quarters. Workmen's compensation was based on the principle of compensating an injured man for loss of earning power following an injury at work and the weekly rate of compensation did not necessarily bear any relation to the severity of the injury. A man who was for the time being incapacitated by some trivial injury would receive the same amount of compensation while the incapacity lasted as the man whose injuries crippled him for life, and if an injured man recovered sufficiently to earn as much as before he was injured compensation would cease, though he might have lost a leg or suffered some other permanent injury. Compensation was the responsibility of the employer and neither the State nor the workman contributed anything towards it. When workmen's compensation came to be examined as part of the review of the social services in 1944 it was generally felt that if the State and the workers were to take part in the administration the scheme would have to be made contributory. The scheme embodied in the National Insurance (Industrial Injuries) Act of 1946 made two main departures from the principles of workmen's compensation. It provided for contributions by employers, workers and the State on the analogy of other schemes of social insurance and placed the administration in the hands of the new Minister of National Insurance. It also completely changed the basis of compensation for industrial injuries by adopting for injuries which persisted beyond a few months, the principles of the war pensions scheme under which the pension depended on the severity of the injury and not on loss of earning power. This alteration in the principles underlying the assessment of compensation, or benefit as it was thenceforth called, was to cause a good many difficulties in the early stages of the

B

new scheme. Although the new scheme was to be contributory, the normal pattern of a contributory scheme, which is to require a substantial qualifying period of employment before benefit is payable, was not adopted, partly because there was no corresponding qualifying period under the Workmen's Compensation Acts it was to replace, but also because the limitation of the benefits to accidents occurring at work provided an automatic link with insurable employment which did not exist in relation to benefits under the main scheme.

NATIONAL INSURANCE

The idea of basing social security on the principle of insurance has a long history. Proposals for compulsory insurance against sickness, infirmity and old age were made in this country as long ago as 1786, but it was a long time before they took practical shape. The first scheme of social insurance to be put into operation was produced in Germany in 1881, but in the 1870s a clergyman named Mr. Blackley had put forward a number of suggestions and from then onwards proposals for pensions and social insurance were constantly being discussed in this country. Social insurance received a setback from the Majority Report of the Royal Commission on the Aged Poor published in 1895. This expressed the view that mutual benefit societies and the Poor Law between them made ample provision against want and that nothing more was needed. The first national pension scheme to reach the statute book was the 5s. old age pension of 1908 but it was not an insurance scheme, being financed wholly out of taxes, and it contained a means test, which was, however, far removed from the destitution test of the Poor Law. The administration of this pension scheme was entrusted to the Revenue Departments largely because they had a local office organization. The scheme embodied some survivals from earlier ideas in the shape of disqualifying people convicted of habitual drunkenness and those who had 'habitually failed to work according to their ability and need'. These pensions became known as 'non-contributory pensions'; about a quarter of a million of them are still being paid but no new non-contributory pensions will be granted to people reaching age 70 after October, 1961. They are now administered by the National Assistance Board.

The first scheme of social insurance was introduced in this country in 1911; it included health insurance, which provided both cash benefits and medical treatment and was administered through the Friendly and other Approved Societies, and also a limited scheme of unemployment benefit which was administered by the Board of

Trade. Since then the social insurance schemes have been steadily extended and improved, both as regards the numbers covered and the nature and amount of the benefits provided. Unemployment benefit, which started by covering about 2¼ million people, was extended in 1920 to cover about two-thirds of all people in employment and now covers nearly everyone working under a contract of service, irrespective of the amount they earn. Insurance pensions came much later. The first insurance pensions were introduced in 1925 when contributory pensions were provided for widows and for men and women attaining the age of 65. The insurance pension under this scheme only covered the five years between the ages of 65 and 70; after that age the pension became a non-contributory one payable wholly out of the Exchequer, but a person who had been entitled to a contributory pension did not have to undergo the normal means test on attaining 70 as his pension became what was technically known as a 'by virtue' pension, that is to say one which was payable by virtue of the fact that he had paid contributions under the insurance scheme even though those contributions did not include anything towards the cost of the post-70 pension. In 1940 women were given pensions at 60; largely as an alternative to providing an increase in the husband's pension for wives who, as was often the case, had not reached the pension age of 65 and were not therefore entitled to pensions in their own right. These insurance or contributory pensions were paid by the Health Departments, the Ministry of Health and the Department of Health for Scotland, but the contribution records on which payment depended were kept, apart from those of a small number of deposit contributors, by the Approved Societies administering the health insurance scheme.

That in brief was the provision made outside the Poor Law for people who owing to unemployment, sickness, injury or old age were unable to earn their own living when the Coalition Government decided in 1941 to set up a committee to examine the whole structure and see how it could be improved. It was as chairman of this committee that Sir William Beveridge, as he then was, produced the report which became famous throughout the world as the Beveridge Report. This contained a comprehensive plan for what came to be known as social security. The Report contained proposals for a new scheme of workmen's compensation and for combining and improving the existing schemes of social insurance, of which the most important was the conception that pensions and benefits should all be paid at the same 'subsistence' rate. These were based on three assumptions which, as the author said, would have to be adopted if his other proposals were to have their desired effect: full employment, a national health service, and family allowances.

FAMILY ALLOWANCES

The last of these assumptions calls for some comment. Family allowances owe much to Miss Eleanor Rathbone who was for many years a Member of Parliament. She advocated them as a remedy for the conditions disclosed in the Rowntree investigations into poverty in the City of York regarding the amount of poverty due to a combination of low wages and large families. She urged that as the wage system did not take account of the size of the family the additional amount needed to ensure a reasonable standard of living for large families should be provided by a social service. The other main reason advanced for family allowances payable in addition to wages was that the insurance schemes and the Poor Law both provided extra allowances for children where the breadwinner was out of work and there was always a risk that large families might be better off on benefit or relief than when the father was working. These two reasons for introducing a scheme of family allowances were adopted in the Beveridge Report. That Report also discussed the relative advantages of including family allowances in the insurance scheme and financing them wholly out of the Exchequer, and came down in favour of the latter. The idea of a means test was also considered in the Report and rejected on the ground that little money would be saved by any reasonable income limit and in so far as the absence of a limit meant the payment of the allowances to people who did not need them, that was a matter which could be corrected through the machinery of the Income Tax.

THE NEW SOCIAL SECURITY PLANS

On the basis of the recommendations in the Beveridge Report the Coalition Government produced its own proposals and embodied them in two White Papers which were presented to Parliament in 1944 and debated in the autumn of that year. The first measure to reach the statute book was the Bill setting up the Ministry of National Insurance, which received the Royal Assent on the 17th November, 1944. It was introduced under the title of 'a Bill to establish a Ministry of Social Insurance', but during the debates in the Commons exception was taken to the use of the word 'Social'. Sir William Beveridge in his Report had favoured the expression 'Social Insurance' because, as he said, it implied both that the scheme was compulsory and that men stood together with their fellows. The term also implied, he thought, a pooling of risks except in so far as separation of risks served a social purpose. In the course of the debate views were expressed from all sides of the House that the word 'Social' was either meaningless or carried the wrong kind of implication. It was therefore changed to 'National' and the new Ministry became the 'Ministry of National Insurance'.

This Bill was followed by the Family Allowances Bill which was passed into law by the Caretaker Government and was indeed almost the last Act of the war-time Parliament before it was dissolved in the summer of 1945.

When the Labour Government took office in July, 1945, Mr. James Griffiths was appointed as Minister of National Insurance. The Government pressed forward with Bills for giving effect to the scheme of social security for which the nation was eagerly waiting. In the main it adopted the plans prepared by the Coalition Government, but it made a number of important changes in them, especially in rates of benefit. Bills were introduced in 1946 and it fell to Mr. Griffiths to pilot them through the House of Commons. They were passed into law with practically no opposition. The three Acts, the Family Allowances Act, the National Insurance Act and the National Insurance (Industrial Injuries) Act, form the statutory basis for the Ministry's work other than war pensions.

CHAPTER III

War Pensions

*

INTRODUCTORY

THE war pensions administration differs from the rest of the Ministry's work in being concerned with a group of men and women which in comparison with the number dealt with under the insurance schemes is relatively small. This is reflected in several features of the administration which were inherited from the former Ministry of Pensions and have been continued by the combined Ministry. The most important of these features are that the Ministry's responsibilities extend to disabled British ex-service men and women all over the world wherever they may be living and that it runs an extensive welfare service for pensioners and their families.

The system of war pensions, which was first introduced in 1917, sets out to compensate men who, as the result of service in the forces during the two world wars or in peace-time since the second war ended, suffer from disabilities which deprive them, wholly or in part, of their ability to enjoy life as freely and fully as ordinary people of the same age; it covers diseases as well as wounds. There are also special schemes which provide disablement pensions for men who have served in the Mercantile Marine, Civil Defence and similar organizations and for civilians who were disabled as the result of enemy action during the 1939–45 war. Pensions are given to widows and orphans and in certain circumstances to parents. Women members of the forces are eligible for pensions but for simplicity the term 'service men' will be used to cover both service men and service women. In 1956 there were about 600,000 men and women in receipt of disablement pensions and pensions were also being paid to over 160,000 widows and orphans and to about 80,000 parents and other dependants.

The terms and conditions for war pensions are contained in a number of different instruments. Some of these are Prerogative Instruments like the Royal Warrants for the Army; in addition there are Orders in Council and Statutory Orders made under various statutes dealing with the other services. Parliamentary control is also secured by the fact that money for war pensions has to be voted annually and by the usual opportunities for asking questions in Parliament and raising matters on the adjournment.

The broad principle underlying the Royal Warrants is that every disabled man should get a basic pension of an amount depending on the degree of disablement due to his service as assessed by medical examination (with additions for rank) and then if, for a particular man, the condition due to his service has further consequences over and above the stark fact of disablement, if, for example, it makes him permanently incapable of work, he will get additional allowances. These provisions recognize the fact that similar disabilities may have different consequences for different men. Most disability pensioners are in regular work, including quite a number of men assessed at 100 per cent. disabled. All these men draw their pensions in addition to their wages and the fact that disability pensions are paid free of income tax adds considerably to their value.

If a man is married, whether the marriage took place before or after he sustained his disability, he will get an allowance for his wife and children. While he is at work the allowance for a wife will be at the rate of 10s. a week for a man assessed at 100 per cent. with proportionately less in other cases; if the man is unable to work and is getting some other benefit or allowance the allowance for his wife will be increased. The allowances for children vary in the same way.

Additional, or as they are technically called 'supplementary', allowances are paid in a variety of circumstances. An 'unemployability' supplement is payable to the man who, as a result of his disability, is unable to work; this requirement is not applied too literally as earnings up to £52 a year are ignored. The supplement is not restricted to pensioners assessed at 100 per cent. and about one-fifth of them are being paid to pensioners with lower assessments. A 'constant attendance allowance' is payable to a man with a disability assessed at 100 per cent. if the nature of the disability makes it necessary that he should have regular attendance; the allowance is, for example, payable to all men who have lost their sight. A 'comforts allowance' is given to all pensioners in receipt of the unemployability supplement and to those receiving the constant attendance allowance and also in certain other cases to pensioners with very severe multiple injuries; an age allowance is given to those over 65 years of age if their pension assessments are 40 per cent. or more. A clothing allowance is given to pensioners who regularly wear an artificial limb and to others whose disabilities cause extra wear and tear to clothing. Lastly there is the 'allowance for lower standard of occupation' given to pensioners who are able to do some work but who are compelled by their injuries to give up their pre-service occupation and have to take other less well remunerated work.

Where a man is unable to work because he is undergoing treatment for his disability he will get treatment allowances equivalent to pension at the full 100 per cent. rate.

How the severely injured man is helped by these supplementary allowances can be shown by an, admittedly extreme, example. In 1956, when the full rate of the basic pension was 67s. 6d. a week, the really seriously injured ex-private with a wife and two children could, with the various additional allowances, have been drawing £12 0s. 4d. a week free of income tax. At the end of 1956 nearly 37,000 pensioners were in receipt of one or more supplementary allowances other than an addition for wife and children, but only a few hundreds were in receipt of the full amount of supplementation available for the very serious cases.

The basic pension is payable as a matter of legal right and there is an elaborate system of appeals to safeguard the disabled man's rights. The supplementary allowances are discretionary and there is no formal appeal from the Minister's decision on them, but applicants are invited to discuss their difficulties with the War Pensions Committee, who will take up deserving cases with the Department. A list of the current rates of war pensions and allowances is given in Appendix I.

ADMINISTRATION

Now that treatment, hospital care and the supply of artificia. limbs and other necessaries for disabled men come under the control of the Ministry of Health, war pension administration is concerned with three things: the decision of claims to basic pensions, which is quasi legal work, the consideration of the pensioner's condition to determine whether he should be given any of the discretionary allowances (there is no means test), and welfare work among pensioners and their families.

Claims to disablement pensions, which can be made quite inform- ally by writing to the Ministry or at one of the local offices, are decided in the first instance by officers of the Department acting on behalf of the Minister who, on medical questions, are guided by the advice of the medical staff. A claim raises questions of 'entitlement' and 'amount'. To be entitled to a pension a man must have served in the armed forces and he must be suffering from disablement caused by an injury or by disease that is either 'attributable to' his service or 'aggravated by' it. Service in the forces is usually established without much difficulty from the service records. The existence of disability of some kind will be established by a medical examination. Nor, in most cases, is attributability a matter for much doubt, at any rate where the disablement is due to wounds, but sometimes, and especially in cases of disease, or where the claim is based on the 'aggravation' of some disability from which the man was suffering when he joined the service, it can raise very difficult issues. Important changes affecting the onus of proof in matters of entitlement were made in 1943. Formerly the man had to prove beyond reasonable doubt that the disability from which he was suffering was due to his service in the forces. Since 1943 the position has been reversed and once it is established that the man has served in the forces and is suffering from a disablement it will, if he puts in his claim within seven years of the end of his service, be assumed to be due to his service unless the Ministry prove beyond reasonable doubt that it is not. This shifting of the onus of proof has considerably eased the burden on a claimant in establishing his claim to a pension.

In the main, questions of attributability and aggravation are medical questions and as such are determined on the advice of the medical staff in the light of the claimant's medical history and the findings of a medical board. The assessment of the degree of disablement for pension purposes is determined in the same way. There are 77 medical boarding centres in Great Britain and facilities for medical boarding are provided in Northern Ireland, the Republic of Ireland and elsewhere overseas. Medical boards usually consist of two medical practitioners.

The Royal Warrant contains a schedule of assessments for specified injuries, mainly amputations without special features; thus blindness or the loss of both arms would be assessed at 100 per cent., the loss of one leg below the knee at 40–60 per cent. according to the site of amputation. This schedule was reviewed in 1946 following a report by a committee presided over by His Honour Judge Hancock. Disabilities mentioned in the schedule will normally be assessed at the rate laid down but a scheduled assessment of less than 100 per cent. will be increased if there are special circumstances, such as a tender stump which increases the severity of the disability; an injury not specified in the list is assessed by the medical board as a matter of judgment against the background of the list of specified injuries which sets the standard. In 1954 a medical committee under Sir Ernest Rock Carling advised that there was no evidence to support the suggestion that the loss of a limb by amputation had any material effect on a man's expectation of life.

In actual practice injuries of the kind set out in the schedule to the Royal Warrant only account for a small proportion of the disabilities for which pensions are being paid. Two-thirds of the disablement pensions now being paid were awarded for diseases and most of them for diseases which though common to the population at large were decided in the case of the pensioners concerned to be attributable to or aggravated by service in the forces.

The payment of war pensions for disabilities due to ordinary disease is in such strong contrast to the practice under the industrial injuries scheme, as described in Chapter V, that some words of explanation are necessary. There are several factors that make it possible to do for the service man what it has always been regarded as impossible to do for the worker in industry. When a man joins the forces he is medically examined and a record is kept of his medical history from the time he joins the forces to the time he leaves; while in the forces practically his whole life is arranged for him by the service authorities and not merely his working hours; in most cases too his service in the forces lasts for only a few years while he is in the prime of life. These special features of life in the forces make it possible to say whether a man who is suffering from some disability when the time comes for him to be discharged sustained that disability as the result of his service or, if it is shown that he had a similar disability when he joined up, whether it was aggravated by his service. The worker in industry on the other hand is seldom medically examined when he starts work; he only spends about a third of his time at his work and he may go on working to an advanced age when health and strength will begin to decline from natural causes.

APPEAL MACHINERY

A man who is dissatisfied with the Minister's decision on his claim to a pension in respect of service in the 1939–45 war or since it ended, either because the claim has been rejected on grounds of entitlement or because the assessment of disablement is too small, can appeal to a special tribunal. In England and Wales there are two kinds of tribunals, both set up by the Lord Chancellor and both statutory in origin but differently constituted; one of them deals with appeals on entitlement and the other with appeals against assessments. An 'entitlement' tribunal consists of a legal chairman, who is very often a former judge in one of the overseas territories, a medical man and a layman (a woman if the claimant is a woman) who has served in the forces; if the claimant is an officer the lay member must have been an officer and in other cases he must have served in the ranks. An 'assessment' tribunal also consists of three members but in this case there are two medical members, one of whom acts as chairman, and a layman with the qualifications set out

above. There are three entitlement tribunals in England and Wales
and two assessment tribunals and in the five years from 1952–1956
they received nearly 55,000 appeals between them; these tribunals
also hear appeals from pensioners overseas. For pensioners in
Scotland there is one tribunal set up by the Lord President of the
Court of Session which by appropriate changes in personnel hears
both entitlement and assessment appeals. Similar arrangements exist
in Northern Ireland, the tribunal there being set up by the Lord
Chief Justice of Northern Ireland.

These tribunals sit in public unless the chairman otherwise decides
on the ground that questions of public security are involved or if the
claimant asks for a private hearing on the ground that owing to the
nature of the case he would be embarrassed if it were heard in public.
Legal representation is allowed, but the case for the Department is
usually put to the tribunal by one of several ex-service officers of the
Ministry specially trained for the purpose and every effort is made to
avoid the atmosphere of a conflict between two sides. The tribunal
have all the documents before them, including a record of the man's
medical history, and oral evidence may also be given. The tribunal's
decision is usually announced at the end of the hearing and subsequently put into writing; reasons are always given. In assessment
appeals the medical members generally make a clinical examination
of the claimant. There is no power to award costs but the usual
travelling and other expenses are allowed to the appellant and his
witnesses.

Unlike most tribunals a pensions appeal tribunal cannot decide by
a majority. The High Court decided on an appeal in a case where a
claim to a pension had been rejected by the tribunal by a majority,
that, since it was incumbent on the Ministry to establish beyond
reasonable doubt that a disability was not due to service, before a
claim was rejected, the tribunal must be unanimous before it could
reject a claim; the argument being that if one member of the tribunal
dissented from his colleagues there was clearly room for substantial
doubt as to the true verdict. A subsequent decision of the High
Court applied a similar rule of unanimity to the allowance of an
appeal in the claimant's favour.

There is no appeal from the decision of an assessment tribunal but
from an entitlement tribunal an appeal lies on a point of law which,
in England and Wales, is by the legal process known as 'case stated'
to a nominated judge of the High Court whose decision is final, and
in Scotland is to the Court of Session; there are corresponding
arrangements in Northern Ireland. A number of important principles
affecting the rights of claimants have been laid down in the judgments
of these Courts.

Between 1950 and 1955 there have in all been 304 appeals from the decisions of the tribunals: of these 22 were allowed and 96 were remitted for further consideration to the tribunals, in most instances because the appellant had obtained new medical evidence since the tribunal gave its decision.

ORGANIZATION

The work of awarding pensions is done at a central office at Blackpool; an arrangement inherited by the new Ministry from the Ministry of Pensions which there were no reasons for altering when the amalgamation took place as it would have been waste of effort to train the staffs of local offices in the technique of deciding cases which everyone must hope will become fewer as time goes on though for the time being the number of new claims remains surprisingly high. In 1956 there were about 17,000 claims to disablement pensions, 13,000 of which were from men whose service in the forces began after the end of the 1939–45 war.

The work of preparing cases for the appeal tribunals is also done at Blackpool, but appeals to the High Court in England and Wales are dealt with in London by the legal staff who draft the 'case stated' and subsequently instruct Counsel to argue the case in Court. Appeals in Scotland are dealt with by a legal adviser in Edinburgh. The office at Blackpool keeps all the records of pensions granted and prepares and issues the pension order books by means of which pensioners draw their pensions at the Post Office of their choice. The Blackpool office is indeed the counterpart for war pension purposes of Newcastle for national insurance and although it is on a smaller scale it has its own special problems. For example, the very large number of different rates of war pensions makes it impossible to mechanize the work to the same extent as at Newcastle and it is doubtful whether it would, as was at one time contemplated, lead to economy if the work of preparing and issuing war pension order books were combined with work on books required for National Insurance purposes.

The Ministry of Pensions had no local offices comparable to those of the old Ministry of National Insurance, but it did have 80 war pensions offices and local enquiry offices in various parts of the country where claims to pensions and supplementary allowances could be made and medical boards arranged, and where pensioners could discuss their problems with the Ministry's welfare officers. These offices have become part of the regional organization of the new Ministry and, except that they are no longer concerned with medical treatment or the provision of such things as artificial limbs or motor tricycles, for which the Ministry of Health is now responsible, they function in much the same way as before. From the ex-service man's point of view the great advantage of the amalgamation of the two Ministries has been the provision of some 900 extra points of contact in the shape of local offices equipped to receive claims for war pensions and supplementary allowances where pensioners can discuss their problems on the spot. Experience has shown that ex-service men make good use of these offices with which many of them are already familiar as insured contributors under the National Insurance Acts.

PENSIONERS ABROAD

The arrangements regarding pensioners overseas vary. In Northern Ireland war pensions are administered by the Government at Westminster and the Ministry maintains an office in Belfast for the purpose. In the Republic of Ireland the Ministry is responsible for the award and payment of war pensions and also for the general welfare of pensioners and it maintains offices in Dublin and Cork; responsibility for hospital and other treatment in the Republic rests with the British Ministry of Health. In other places overseas the Ministry is responsible not only for pensions and welfare but also for arranging medical treatment when required; most of the work is done through a local agent, who may be an officer of the local war pensions administration or, in a foreign country, the local British Consul, but an office is still maintained in Ottawa for pensioners in North America. In 1956 there were about 45,000 pensioners overseas for whom the Ministry was responsible and about one-quarter of them were in Canada and the United States of America. The Canadian office of the Ministry also acts as paymaster for other United Kingdom departments paying pensions in North America; it is paying about 5,000 national insurance pensions and about 3,000 other pensions of various kinds.

SPECIAL SCHEMES

Other kinds of war pensions are payable to men and women, or their dependants, who became casualties in the 1939–45 war although they did not serve with the armed forces of the Crown. These pensions have been awarded under various schemes made by the Minister under statutory authority.

Among the schemes prepared against the outbreak of war were several providing pensions for men who were injured, or to their dependants if they were killed, while serving in the Merchant Navy and the Sea Fishing Services, the Naval Auxiliary Forces and Pilot and Light Vessels and Sea Salvage Services. These pensions, of which there are about 15,000 still in payment, are statutory in origin but the regulations governing their payment are closely modelled on the Royal Warrants for war pensions.

A further scheme provided pensions for civilians injured in air raids or for their dependants if they were killed. It had its origin in the difficulties which it was foreseen would occur if men and women were injured or killed while working in the factories and workshops. It was essential to the war effort that they should continue to work as long as possible in spite of enemy attacks, but it was considered inappropriate, and indeed it would have been unjust, to expect their employers to compensate them under the provisions of the Workmen's Compensation Acts. Emergency legislation passed on the outbreak of war accordingly excluded the payment of workmen's compensation in cases of injury due to enemy action and arranged instead for the payment of pensions similar to those provided by the Royal Warrants for the services. The Personal Injuries (Civilians) Scheme was thus in some ways the forerunner of the Industrial Injuries Scheme described in Chapter V. In addition to compensation for war injuries to the civilian population the scheme provided compensation to Civil Defence Workers, including the Fire Service, for war service injuries sustained in the course of their duties. About 48,000 awards were made under the scheme, of which about 24,000 were still in payment in 1956. These figures are very much smaller than was expected when the scheme was devised.

There is also a special scheme for former members of the Polish Forces who served under British command or in the Polish Resettlement Corps, under which 5,500 pensions were still being paid in 1956, of which about 500 were to the widows and other dependants.

The schemes so far mentioned related to the 1939–45 war and were based on and analogous to the Royal Warrants for the Army. The Ministry also administers one other scheme of a very different character. When a man is called up for national service or, as a reservist, is recalled to the forces for more than 13 days, he can claim a special allowance payable to his family known as a National Service Grant. These grants are the peace-time equivalent of the War Service Grants introduced during the last war. They originated in the hardships caused by the absence with the forces of a wage-earner in cases where the loss of wages was not adequately compensated for by the service pay and allowances. The grants are administered by the Ministry as agents for the Service Departments who are responsible for the rules governing eligibility. They involve enquiries into the families' resources and their needs and these enquiries are made on behalf of the Service Departments by the

local officers of the National Assistance Board. The object of a
grant is to help the man, within certain limits, to meet his family
obligations and other commitments.

The number of War Service or National Service Grants in payment
reached about half a million in 1944; by the end of 1955 they had
fallen to about 9,000 but the numbers increased again to about
11,700 in 1956 as a result of the Suez emergency.

WELFARE AND CHILDREN'S WORK

For several years before the two Ministries were amalgamated, the
Ministry of Pensions had made a special feature of welfare work for
the war disabled and their families and for the widows and dependants of those who died as a result of war service. Welfare officers
were appointed in 1948 at all the main Ministry of Pensions offices
throughout the country and at the hospitals then administered by
the Pensions Department. In addition to this welfare service the
Minister had statutory duties to fulfil on behalf of children orphaned
through the war. Both these services have been continued by the
new Ministry and the welfare officers still keep in close touch with
pensioners in hospital.

It is not easy to describe in a few words just what work is done by
a welfare service. The need for such a service arises from the complexity of modern life and the number of statutory and voluntary
services which exist to assist those in need of help. The ordinary
person overcome by some misfortune does not know which way to
turn. He may have a vague idea that he could get help from some
local authority or from the National Health Service or from a
voluntary agency, but he does not know where to find them or to
whom to apply. For the disabled ex-service man the demands of
civilian existence are likely to present themselves in even more
forbidding guise and without a friendly hand he may find himself
quite unable to cope with them. The welfare officer can do much
both to help the pensioner get his problems into perspective and to
put him on the right road. Particular attention is paid through the
welfare service to the rehabilitation and resettlement of the disabled
and to the encouragement of self-reliance. The welfare worker must
make himself thoroughly familiar with all the services available
both locally and nationally to help his clients. He must establish and
maintain contact with the people who actually run the services and
know how to put the pensioner or widow in need of help in touch
with the appropriate ones. When, as is often the case, it is necessary
to enlist several services at once, the welfare officer can act as a
co-ordinating link. Little of the work is spectacular or concerned

with the big affairs of life but the help given can often make all the difference to the man struggling to accustom himself to the consequences of his disability.

Special arrangements have been made for War Pensions Committee members and their associated voluntary workers to visit pensioners who are so severely disabled as to be unemployable. Through these visitors, efforts are also made to interest the severely disabled in homecrafts and hobbies which will help them pass their days in as constructive and agreeable a way as possible. The Ministry's home-craft service has done a great deal for these men. It works in close co-operation with voluntary societies, and with the additional help of a small team of handicraft instructors arranges for men to be trained in various crafts such as leather work, basket work, weaving, etc., ensuring also that they are supplied with the materials and tools they require. None of this is done as a commercial venture but every effort is made to assist pensioners to sell the work which they produce and which they cannot dispose of locally; in a recent year sales of homecrafts totalled over £11,000 and the whole sum was handed to the men concerned. Some of the pensioners who took up homecrafts as a hobby have reached such a high degree of skill that they have been able to undertake full-time employment or set up businesses of their own.

In addition to this scheme, special attention is also paid to the needs of elderly war widows. Every widow attaining 70 years of age is asked whether she would like a visitor, and if she accepts this invitation a call is arranged either by a War Pensions Committee member or voluntary worker, or by a member of the several voluntary organizations which co-operate in this scheme. It has been found that much practical help can be given through these visits, and they are valuable in alleviating loneliness.

In fulfilment of the Minister's responsibilities a great deal of work is done among war orphans and for this purpose the Ministry main-tains a staff of children's officers. There are over 4,000 orphans most of whom have lost both their parents. Many are living with relatives, some are with foster parents and some are living with widowed mothers in conditions which occasionally give rise to some anxiety about their well-being. Children's officers take a close personal interest in the children under their charge. They visit them regularly and when the time comes for a child to start work they co-operate with juvenile employment officers in choosing a suitable job for the child. In many cases a real personal friendship has sprung up and contact is retained long after the child has become settled in a life of its own. There are also a small number of handicapped children to whom special attention is given and on whose behalf all the various specialized services are enlisted by co-operation between the children's and welfare officers.

ADVISORY COMMITTEES

There are a number of advisory bodies attached to the Ministry in connection with war pensions administration. Attached to Headquarters in London there is the Central Advisory Committee of which the Minister and both the Parliamentary Secretaries are members, as well as the Permanent Secretary. The Committee includes several Members of Parliament specially interested in war pension questions, representatives of several of the ex-service organizations and of voluntary bodies working among ex-service men, and also several chairmen of local War Pensions Committees. It was first set up under the War Pensions Act, 1921, to consider any matters connected with war pensions which the Minister refers to it for advice. It deals with general questions and not with individual cases and meets periodically to review outstanding problems affecting the welfare of ex-service men and the administration of pensions. When matters relating to hospital treatment, artificial limbs, tricycles and motor cars for disabled men became the responsibility of the Health Departments it was arranged that any views the Committee might express on such questions would be forwarded to the appropriate Department. An observer from the Health Departments now attends meetings when such matters are to be discussed.

Another central body is the Special Grants Committee established in 1917 to advise on certain types of individual cases. The chairman of this Committee is a lawyer and the other members are persons nominated by the Minister as being specially interested in war pension matters. Its work is now limited to the consideration of individual cases where a question has arisen whether a widow is worthy to continue to receive a pension.

There are 155 local War Pensions Committees altogether in Great Britain and there is also a Committee for Northern Ireland. These Committees are composed of men and women appointed by the Minister from among people in the locality who are known to take an interest in war pensioners and their problems. In addition to advising on general questions affecting the administration in their area, War Pensions Committees investigate the cases of individual pensioners. They are specially concerned with complaints about the withholding, or the withdrawal, of supplementary allowances. Pensioners are told that if they are in difficulties over their pensions or allowances they can apply to their local War Pensions Committee for help and advice, and frequently Committees with their

C

knowledge of local conditions and circumstances are able to bring additional facts to the notice of the Ministry that justify a review in the pensioner's favour of a previously adverse decision. They are also the focus of much of the local welfare work among pensioners and they maintain panels of people willing to visit pensioners and try to help them in their difficulties. As a matter of administration local War Pensions Committees come under the Ministry's Regional Controllers and officers from regional headquarters frequently attend their meetings. The Minister keeps in close touch with the work of the Committees and attends periodical meetings of the chairmen at convenient regional centres at which matters affecting the welfare of war pensioners and their dependants are discussed.

CHAPTER IV

National Insurance

*

GENERAL

THE largest of the schemes administered by the Ministry is the national insurance scheme embodied in the National Insurance Act, 1946, which makes provision for a number of different pensions and benefits. When he was introducing the White Papers setting out the Coalition Government's proposals for their new Social Security Programme, Sir William Jowitt (as he then was), who afterwards became the first Minister of National Insurance, pointed out that the main proposals were far from novel as unemployment and sickness benefit, maternity benefit and pensions for the aged and for widows had been provided for many years through earlier schemes. What the new Act did was to bring all these schemes together and make a number of changes in the extent of cover provided, in the rules for benefit and pensions and in the arrangements for administering them; but the old schemes and the way in which they had been administered left many marks on the new forms that were to replace them.

The new scheme was universal and there were no personal exemptions other than a 'small income exception' for those who could not afford to be insured; pensions would no longer be granted on grounds of age alone but only when people retired from work, and increments, that would add materially to the value of the pension, would be given to those who deferred their retirement; instead of a small pension granted automatically to every widow the Act provided an elaborate system of widow's benefits based on the principle that long-term benefits should only be paid to widows with children to look after and to widows incapable of work through age or infirmity. Changes were made in the contribution conditions for unemployment benefit; the rate for sickness benefit was brought up to the level of unemployment benefit and pensions; the lower rate of disablement benefit for long-term sickness was abolished and all medical treatment benefits became matters for the National Health Service. Increases for dependants would also be payable with sickness benefit as they had for years been paid with unemployment benefit. The principle of reducing benefits if the claimant's contribution record was deficient, which had been the rule for sickness benefit, was extended to cover unemployment benefit and pensions. It was decided to concentrate responsibility for all the various benefits and pensions, which had formerly been shared between the Ministry of Labour and the Ministry of Health, in a new Ministry. The administration of sickness benefit through Approved Societies was discontinued but unemployment benefit continued to be paid through the agency of the Employment Exchanges.

A complete list of the pensions and benefits provided by the National Insurance Act, the current rates of pension and benefits and the main conditions which have to be satisfied before they are payable are set out in Appendix II, and as this book is not intended to be a guide to national insurance we shall only concern ourselves with points that have required special attention or given rise to special problems in administration.

UNIVERSALITY

The old schemes had applied to manual workers who worked under a contract of service and to non-manual workers under a contract of service who did not earn more than £420 a year. Even within these limits whole industries were left outside, in part or in whole, on the ground that adequate provision was made for the employees in some other way. The new scheme applied to everyone. The main result of this was to bring into insurance many people in the higher income groups for whom compulsory insurance was a novelty, and some of them were inclined to be critical of rules and regulations which others more accustomed to national insurance accepted as natural in a State scheme. Among the new groups included for the first time were people working on their own account or, as they were called, the 'self-employed' who had no employer with whom the responsibilities of state insurance could be shared and also a small group of people who had no regular work of any kind—the 'non-employed'. It was not thought possible to insure the self-employed against unemployment, for many of them were able, within wide limits, to choose when and under what conditions they would do their work, and as the main purpose of the scheme was to provide insurance against loss of earnings neither unemployment nor sickness benefit was provided for the small non-employed group. These considerations led to the creation of the different classes of insured persons described in Chapter VII each of which pays different contributions for a different group of benefits. Within each category the scheme is universal in the sense that everyone pays the same rate of contribution regardless of their personal circumstances, unless exempted on poverty grounds, and everyone draws the same rate of benefit irrespective of their earnings when at work. In this respect the national insurance scheme differs from schemes in many foreign countries where benefits are related to earnings and contributions vary accordingly. The scheme is often described as one providing flat-rate benefits in return for flat-rate contributions, but the rate of benefits may vary in several ways. If the claimant has a deficient contribution record his benefit or pension will be reduced; if he continues at work beyond the minimum pension age his pension may be increased. The payment of increases for dependants, although the married man pays no more than the single man, might also be regarded as a departure from the strict rule of equal benefits for equal contributions. Again, while married women are entitled to choose whether they will be insured or not when they are working, if they do decide to insure their sickness and unemployment benefits will be paid at a lower rate than the standard rate for other women.

SICKNESS BENEFIT

There are seldom less than 800,000 people on sickness benefit at any one time and the payment of their benefit constitutes the main work of the Ministry's local offices. The volume of this work has remained remarkably constant from year to year. Taking as a measure the number of fresh claims to sickness benefit received in the local offices, we find that over the whole period up to the end of 1956 the average number of claims has been in the neighbourhood of 140,000 a week. Comparing one year with another the weekly average has only once fallen below 133,000 and only once risen above 150,000; the lowest figure was 126,700 for 1952 and the highest 180,000 for 1957. Nor, comparing one month with another, does the number of claims received vary as much as might have been expected with the seasons of the year. The monthly average rarely falls much below 100,000 a week and seldom rises much above 200,000; in the two years 1952 and 1953, for example, the monthly average only fell below 90,000 in one month, July, 1952, and only rose above 200,000 in the two months of January and February, 1953. Apart from epidemics the variations in the amount of sickness benefit work in the local offices do not give rise to much difficulty.

An influenza epidemic is a very different matter and can give rise to serious problems for the Ministry. The worst experience so far was during the severe epidemic in the autumn of 1957, when over 500,000 fresh claims were received in each of three successive weeks. By way of comparison, the number of claims never rose above 200,000 in any week in 1952 and even in 1953, when there was an epidemic in the spring, the highest number of fresh claims in any week was only just over 275,000. The number of fresh claims to sickness benefit thus provides a useful barometer for measuring the pressure of work in the local offices.

January and February are always anxious months for the Ministry and the medical staff keep a careful look-out for any signs or information which might suggest that an influenza epidemic was imminent. A weekly intake of anything approaching 500,000 fresh claims places a very severe strain on the staff and plans have to be made well in advance to cope with any emergency. Fortunately for the organization, epidemics seldom strike every part of the country at the same time so that during an epidemic some offices will be strained almost to breaking-point while others are experiencing more or less normal conditions. In one week in the spring of 1953, for example, more than 120 offices received over three times their usual number of fresh claims, but 80 of these offices were in the two London regions and 35 more in the neighbouring Eastern and Southern regions. None of the offices in the Northern or Western regions were unduly pressed. This makes it possible in case of need to reinforce hard-pressed offices by staff drawn from less seriously affected parts of the country. In an emergency the normal procedure in a local office may be modified by omitting some of the checks normally imposed and by postponing less urgent work; though it is noticeable that managers of local offices are reluctant to resort to the postponement of work if it can possibly be avoided as it tends to prolong the period of strain by piling up work that must be done eventually. The difficulties of offices receiving an exceptionally large number of claims are usually increased by the fact that as their staff live in the affected area many of them will become casualties and the office will be faced with the double burden of a depleted staff and a large increase in the work.

The procedure for claiming sickness benefit is simple. The claim form is incorporated with the medical certificate which is the normal evidence of incapacity. On receipt of a claim the office will check the contribution record; in many cases it will be known already as the result of a previous claim, but if not it will be obtained from Newcastle by means of a 'shuttle card', the purpose and use of which are described in the section in Chapter IX dealing with the Newcastle office. On receipt of a second medical certificate, usually a week later, showing the claimant has been ill for a period, the amount due will be computed and payment made, generally by means of a postal draft which the claimant can cash at a Post Office, though in a few cases the claimant may prefer to get payment in cash by calling at, or sending a representative to, the local office of the Ministry.

If the claimant has a wife and children he can claim an increase of benefit on their account by placing a mark in the appropriate place on the claim form. This will be followed by a request from the local office for further information on such points as the age of the children and whether the wife is working (if she is earning more than 40s. a week she cannot be treated as a dependant).

If a claim to benefit, or at least a notice of sickness, is not sent within the three days allowed by the regulations, benefit may be withheld for the early days of sickness, unless the claimant can show he had good cause for not giving notice or making a claim in time; but since 1950 a special concession has been made to people claiming benefit for the first time, in whose case 21 days are allowed. Late claims were frequent in the early days and some people, who had never belonged to a friendly society, from whom the idea of a time limit was copied, and had never been insured under the old National Health Insurance Scheme, resented being deprived of benefit under the rule. It is not always easy to decide what should be regarded as good cause for delay, but it was not long before the National Insurance Commissioner, faced with the simple plea of ignorance of the rules, felt bound to decide that this could not be accepted as a valid reason for not obeying them. As more and more people have occasion to claim benefit, knowledge of the rules spreads and cases of difficulty are less frequent than they were in the early days.

Most of the 7 million spells of sickness for which benefit is paid every year last less than three weeks, but at any one time there are always about 250,000 people who have been continuously in receipt of benefit for long periods. In their case medical certificates, instead of being required every week, may only be called for at longer intervals, and many of them receive their benefit by means of order books similar to those used for pensions.

The existence of so many people on sickness benefit makes it necessary to take steps to check the genuineness of incapacity in cases where the period of absence from work seems unduly prolonged in view of the nature of the illness disclosed by the medical certificates. Two kinds of checks are used. Claimants are visited by sick visitors on the staff of the Ministry and cases are referred to Regional Medical Officers of the Health Departments for medical examination and report. Before calling a man for examination the Regional Medical Officer consults the man's own doctor; this avoids any possibility of people who are seriously ill being worried by unnecessary medical examinations. Moreover if the man's own doctor disagrees with the view of the Regional Medical Officer a third opinion will be obtained. The volume of this work is considerable. In 1956 over 600,000 claimants were visited and over 620,000 were referred for further medical examination. Experience extending over many years, including the experience of Approved Societies under the earlier scheme, goes to show that out of every 100 people referred for further examination, some 20 send in final certificates, about 18 do not bother to attend and their benefit automatically ceases, about 12 attend and are declared fit for work and the remaining 50 continue on benefit.

In the early days of the new scheme fears were expressed that the increased rates of benefit were leading to increased absenteeism on medical certificates, but elaborate tests did not disclose any serious abuse except perhaps in a few instances where employers were paying full wages to people who were away sick without making any deduction for sickness benefit. What constitutes incapacity through sickness must in marginal cases be a matter of opinion and opinions may well differ, but while the reliability of medical certificates must always be a matter of concern to the Ministry there is no evidence of any serious abuse of the scheme, and indeed the volume of sickness benefit claims has so far been substantially less than was originally forecast by the Government Actuary.

UNEMPLOYMENT BENEFIT

The day-to-day administration of unemployment benefit, the taking and deciding of claims and the payment of benefit, is carried on by the Employment Exchanges of the Ministry of Labour and National Service as agents for the Ministry of Pensions and National Insurance: its details therefore lie outside the scope of this book. The essential feature of the procedure for paying unemployment benefit is that the claimant has to attend personally during ordinary working hours and sign a register as proof of unemployment and when he attends at the Exchange his availability for work can be tested by the offer of a suitable job. This links up with the 'placing' or 'vacancy' work of the Exchanges and it is for this reason that the administration of unemployment benefit has been left with them. This example of agency work by one Department on behalf of another has worked very well.

The Ministry of Pensions and National Insurance is responsible for all questions of policy connected with unemployment benefit including proposals for modifying the conditions under which it is payable, and the Ministry also provides the Exchanges with the necessary details of a claimant's contribution record to enable them to decide claims. In a period of full employment questions relating to unemployment benefit have not occupied the public mind to anything like the extent they did during the inter-war years. The questions with which the Ministry has been concerned have mainly related to the conditions under which benefit is paid in marginal cases such as seasonal workers and workers whose hours of work do not fit into the normal pattern of employment. People who regularly work for short periods of the year in some seasonal employment have always been difficult to fit into the unemployment benefit scheme as it has always been recognized that the Insurance Fund should not be used to encourage employees to organize their work on a part-time or seasonal basis. Under the old scheme the Seasonal Workers Regulations attained some notoriety and one of the first questions referred to the National Insurance Advisory Committee for advice was how these workers should be treated for unemployment benefit purposes. After prolonged consideration the Committee recommended in effect that benefit should not as a general rule be payable to a seasonal worker outside the season when he normally expected to be working.

A somewhat similar question concerned the insurance against unemployment of men known as 'share fishermen'. These are men who join together to run a small fishing craft and are remunerated by a share of the profits. They have no employer, being rather partners in a joint venture, and they are not therefore within the scope of the unemployment benefit scheme. Strong representations were made that they should be provided for and the problem was referred to the National Insurance Advisory Committee who eventually succeeded in working out a scheme to cover them. This was put into force and is now being operated, though not without many difficulties which serve to emphasize how hard it is to provide unemployment benefit for men who have no employer to direct when and how they are to work.

Although what was known as 'extended benefit' is now a thing of the past, it is worth while giving a short account of it especially as its administration involved a novel use of the local tribunals. A large part of the chequered history of unemployment benefit has been concerned with the period for which a person should be entitled to draw benefit without having to comply with some condition that was not imposed on the man who has only been unemployed for a short period. The ordinary rule has always been that a man who draws more than a certain number of days of benefit must requalify by a period of work before he can draw any more, but if he has a long spell of steady work behind him then the period for which he can draw benefit is extended by what are known as 'added days', the number of which is related by a mathematical formula to the number of contributions paid over the last few years and the amount of benefit he has recently drawn.

In 1946, when the National Insurance Bill was passing through Parliament, both parties were committed to the policy of full employment and there was considerable discussion about whether in these circumstances an unlimited period of benefit should not be allowed to those individuals who failed to secure work. In the end a limit was fixed and the rules for additional days were modified and re-enacted. The proposal made in the Beveridge Report that people who remained unemployed for long periods should be required to undergo training was rejected on the ground that it would bring training into disrepute if it were treated as a test of genuine unemployment or imposed as a penalty. Notwithstanding the acceptance of the policy of 'full employment' it was feared that the transition from a war to a peace footing might lead to serious unemployment in certain areas and the idea of leaving men thus affected to assistance and the means test was politically unacceptable. To meet this contingency the Act contained a temporary provision, to run for five years, under which people who had exhausted their rights to ordinary benefit might be given as many extra days as were recommended by a local tribunal after considering the applicant's individual record and circumstances (other than financial circumstances, because there was no means test), the industrial conditions of the district where he lived and any general directions issued by the Minister. The administrative novelty of this provision was that the local tribunal, which normally sits to interpret the law as laid down by the Act and regulations, was acting in a purely administrative capacity. The Minister's directions were very general in character and were concerned with such questions as whether the applicant was prepared to accept work outside his usual occupation, to undergo training or to move to some place where work could be found for him. In considering whether to recommend extended benefit in a particular case the tribunal was not trying to decide whether a claimant fulfilled strictly-worded conditions like those which governed the payment of ordinary benefit, but whether on the whole his continued unemployment could be said to be due to the war or other circumstances outside his own control. The Insurance Fund was safeguarded by the provision that extended benefit was to be paid out of the Exchequer and not out of the fund.

The fears that had inspired the provision were never realized. Employment remained good everywhere and the number of people on extended benefit never rose above 55,000 at any time. The provision lapsed on the 5th July, 1953, and during the six years for which extended benefit was paid about half a million new claims were made but many claimants received it for comparatively short periods only and then found work. Careful records were kept of what happened to those who were actually drawing the benefit when it came to an end and these showed that many of them were very doubtfully within the category for which it was intended. Most of them found work and of the rest all, except a very small number, received as much from some other social service as they had been getting while on benefit. It cannot be said that this latest attempt to find a half-way house between insurance benefit paid subject to strictly defined conditions and assistance subject to a test of personal need was a success.

A number of questions affecting unemployment benefit have been referred to the National Insurance Advisory Committee for advice, including such matters as the scope of the rule that a man must be available for work and the payment of benefit for very short spells of unemployment. In 1957 the Act was amended to limit a short-time worker's title to benefit for days on which he does not normally work. Generally, however, few changes have been made in the conditions for payment of benefit laid down in 1946, which themselves largely follow the pre-war rules.

RETIREMENT PENSIONS

Since 1948 retirement pensions have taken the place of unemployment benefit as the major problem of social insurance. This is due partly to the absence of large-scale unemployment and partly to the rapid growth in the number of people reaching pensionable age. The substitution for the old age pension of a retirement pension with its corollaries the earnings rule and increments for deferred retirement has considerably increased the complexities of pension administration. When a pension was granted automatically to people as soon as they attained pensionable age, subject only to their contribution record being in order, it was usually a simple matter to decide, once and for all, whether the conditions were fulfilled and if a pension was granted all that was left for the administration to do was to renew the pension order book from time to time. The claimant's contribution record is still important under the new scheme and it has indeed taken on an added significance because, if it is deficient, the pension may be paid at a reduced rate. The claimant's age must also be checked, not only to make sure that he has reached the minimum pension age, 65 for a man (60 for a woman), but also because, if he is over that age, he may be entitled to a pension increased by one or more increments for deferred retirement. Finally, it is necessary to decide whether the claimant has retired. In most cases this will not be difficult as he will have given up work entirely or taken up some quite different work of a kind which, in the language of the Act, 'is not inconsistent with retirement'; many people have in fact been able to qualify for a retirement pension even though they are regularly working in some small job of a kind suitable for people who have retired from regular work. Difficulties do, however, arise in connection with people like the self-employed shop-keeper who continues in his normal business but as time goes on takes less and less part in running it, or cleaners or jobbing gardeners who simply reduce the number of working days as they get older until perhaps only a nominal amount of work is being done. It is not easy to say in cases like these precisely at what point retirement takes place. It was to provide a general rule for such cases that in the very early days of the scheme the Unemployment Insurance Umpire, who for a short while carried out the functions of the National Insurance Comissioner before the latter was appointed, laid down the rule that in general a person who did more than twelve hours' work a week could not be regarded as retired. The Act had declared that a person doing some work might be regarded as retired so long as the work he did was 'inconsiderable in amount' and twelve hours a week was the measure adopted for this purpose.

Even when it has been decided that a person has retired and a pension has been awarded, the administration still has to ensure that the pension is appropriately adjusted if he earns more than the prescribed amount in any week. Once a pensioner reaches 70, if a man, or 65 if a woman, the retirement condition and with it the earnings rule cease to apply and the pension becomes an unconditional one. The great majority of pensioners are over these ages and in December, 1955, it was estimated that out of a total of $4\frac{1}{2}$ million pensioners only 420,000 men and 630,000 women would have been within the scope of the earnings rule had they been working and less than 40,000 actually had their pensions reduced by earnings.

The administration of retirement pensions is shared between the Central Office at Newcastle and the local offices. The Central Office keeps track of everyone approaching minimum pension age and informs the appropriate local office which sends out a notice inviting a provisional application for a pension. By this means the formal work of checking age and contribution records can be done before the minimum age of retirement is reached. This not only enables a pension to be put into payment quickly when the pensioner does retire but also ensures a regular flow of work in the Central Pensions Branch. When a man decides to retire he has to send a notice of retirement to the local office, who make any enquiries necessary to satisfy themselves that retirement has taken place; the local office will also be responsible for operating the earnings rule once a pension is awarded. If no notice of retirement is received before the age of 70 for a man (65 for a woman) a claim will be invited. The Central Office is responsible for the preparation and issue of the order books by means of which the pensioner draws his pension. These books usually contain 52 orders at the appropriate rate and bear the pensioner's name and address and pension number. They are sent by the Central Office to a Post Office nominated for the purpose by the pensioner and the pensioner then calls at the Post Office and collects his book. This arrangement has been proved by long experience to be more satisfactory than sending the book to the pensioner's private address; it leads to fewer order books going astray and it makes it possible to send out the renewal book well in advance of the expiry of the old one, thus avoiding any risks of a gap in the regularity of payments without giving rise to the confusion which the possession by the pensioner of two books might cause. Pension orders are dated consecutively and no order can be cashed before the date it bears; as a general rule they must be cashed by the pensioner himself but provision is made for payment to a deputy nominated in writing by the pensioner.

As over 250 million pension orders are used every year the printing and assembling of the orders is a lengthy business. They have to be printed on special security paper to prevent forgery and there is only a limited number of machines that can do the work. Books of orders run for twelve months and about 100,000 books are issued every week.

A change in the rate of pension is a major operation for the Department. Not only must new books be printed at the new rate but all the outstanding books in the hands of pensioners, except those which happen to expire on or near the date fixed for the new rate to come into force, have to be up-rated. To issue new books to every pensioner to start on the same day, even if it were physically possible to do so, would disrupt the course of administration which depends on a regular flow of books falling due for renewal week by week. A variety of measures therefore have to be adopted to make certain that at the Appointed Day every pensioner will have in his possession an order book on which he can draw his pension at the new rate, and these measures have to be carefully timed. Preliminary steps have to be taken long before any public announcement of a change in the rate of pension is made and at the earliest possible date a start is made with the printing of the new books. This is a crucial decision because once printing at the old rate is stopped and printing at the new rate begins it would be very difficult to preserve continuity of payment at the old rate. When the day for bringing the new rate into force is fixed an elaborate programme of work is drawn up. On the Appointed Day, whatever it is, there will be a large number of current books in the hands of pensioners and all except those due for renewal on or about that day will have to be up-rated by over-stamping. To ensure smooth progress of the work and to avoid queuing, pensioners are asked to bring or send their books to the local office in accordance with a time-table based on the initial letter of their names. When the pensioner brings his book in it is over-stamped on the spot and the pensioner takes it away with him; when a book is sent by post especially careful timing is needed if delays in payment are to be avoided because it has to be sent in, over-stamped and returned to the pensioner in the course of one week between one pension pay day and the next. Pensioners have always co-operated well in these arrangements and with the practice local offices have had from repeated changes in rates of pension they are getting very familiar with the arrangements.

The work in the local office is only one part of the business. As order books are being sent out week by week by the Central Office special steps have to be taken to ensure that any book for a period which straddles the Appointed Day for the new rate contains the correct number of orders at the old rate and the correct number at the new. This involves the Central Office in a large operation of up-rating existing stocks of books and it is a complicated business because the make-up of each weekly batch of books differs from the preceding one. About 500,000 books are dealt with in this way by the Central Office on each change of rate. Finally, care is needed to ensure that all batches of new books which start on or after the Appointed Day are at the new rate and as renewal books are sent out some two to three weeks before they will be needed this too is more complicated than might appear. Suggestions have been made from time to time that to shorten the period between the announcement of an increase in the rate of pensions and the day fixed for bringing it into force, a period which is at present largely governed by the time required to print new books, a simple instruction might be issued to the Post Office to pay at the higher rate. This suggestion has been examined several times and dismissed as impracticable on the ground of the uncertainty and confusion which would arise, especially in crowded Post Offices, if payment was made at some rate other than that stated on the pension order forms.

An earnings rule of some kind is an essential part of the arrangements for a retirement pension but it is a difficult thing to administer satisfactorily. Some pensioners—perhaps finding that retirement is not all they expected—go back to a regular job, and earn so much that they cannot draw their pensions. They return their pension order books to the Ministry and when they have done this they need not bother to declare earnings week by week. At any one time, about 20,000 pensioners surrender their order books in this way. Other pensioners, who work regularly but for earnings which leave part of their pension in payment, have their order books adjusted for a period in advance. Where an order book has not been adjusted in anticipation of regular earnings the pensioner cannot sign or cash the order in any week when he earns more than the prescribed amount. He must then take the book to the local office for adjustment as the Post Office cannot undertake to make adjustments on the spot. It has sometimes been suggested that instead of treating earnings on a weekly basis they should be averaged over a period. It is perhaps worth pointing out how much more complicated such an arrangement would be for the pensioner, who would have to declare all earnings however small to enable the average to be struck, and for the local office who would have to keep a running record of pensioners' earnings.

The form of the earnings rule was substantially altered in 1956 following an exhaustive report on the whole question by the National Insurance Advisory Committee. Under the old rule a pension would be reduced by the full amount of any earnings in excess of the prescribed amount in any week. This figure was originally 20s.; it was raised to 40s. in 1951 but the general character of the rule remained the same. In 1956 the amount a pensioner could earn without affecting his pension was raised to 50s. a week and the rule was altered to provide that for earnings between 50s. and 70s. only sixpence is deducted for every shilling earned over 50s. Where earnings exceed 70s., 10s. is deducted for the earnings between 50s. and 70s. and one shilling is deducted for each shilling earned over 70s. Under this rule a man can earn up to £5 10s. a week before he loses his pension entirely.

Another change in the retirement arrangements was also recommended by the Committee. Under the original Act retirement was an irrevocable act and once a man retired he lost for ever the chance of earning increments on his pension by continuing to work after reaching 65. When the amount of the increment was raised in 1951 people who had retired were given for a limited period an option to resume work and thus start qualifying for the new increments; a step to which the name of 'de-retire' was unfortunately applied. Very few pensioners took advantage of this provision but pressure to allow 'de-retirement' continued and the Committee accordingly recommended that the option should be made general and that anyone who has retired should be able to resume work and qualify for increments. A Bill giving effect to this recommendation was passed in the spring of 1956.

WIDOWS

The 1946 Act completely altered the provision made for widows. Under the earlier Acts, a widow was given a pension of 10s. a week for life, or so long as she remained a widow, with a children's allowance of 5s. for the first and 3s. for each subsequent child. This pension, which was neither large enough to maintain a widow nor really needed as an addition to wages earned by the widow in full-time employment, was replaced by a far more elaborate system. The idea underlying the new provision was that every widow should get a substantial benefit immediately following her husband's death to tide her over the inevitable period of adjustment, but that only widows with children or those unable because of age or illness to go out to work should get long-term benefits.

A description of these benefits, as modified by subsequent legislation following a review by the National Insurance Advisory Committee, is given in Appendix I, but in brief they comprise a widow's allowance for 13 weeks if the husband dies before retiring from work; a widowed mother's allowance granted to widows with children so long as the children are under 18; and a widow's pension payable to a widow over 50 years of age when her husband dies or, if she has been getting a widowed mother's allowance, when the last child reaches 18. Widows are also given special credits to enable them to qualify for sickness and unemployment benefit if they are not entitled to any other benefit. Widow's benefits, other than the widow's allowance, are subject to an earnings rule and in certain cases the widow must have been married for at least three years before her husband's death.

This system of widow's benefit naturally involves much more detailed administration than the old 10s. pension which was awarded on the husband's death and was not subject to an earnings rule. Under the old scheme, once the pension was granted the Department was only concerned with the possibility of re-marriage or cohabitation, in which case the pension would cease. Now there are three different kinds of benefits and two of them have earnings rules. For many years to come, moreover, there will be widows drawing one of the new benefits with an earnings rule who also have a reserved right to the old 10s. pension without an earnings rule, and in administering such cases care must be taken in applying the earnings rule not to reduce the pension below 10s. There are others who qualify for the old 10s. pension and not for the new benefits; at the end of 1956 there were about 130,000 of these cases. The administration of widow's benefits, most of which falls on the local offices, accordingly calls for considerable care over details if mistakes are to be avoided. In 1956 there were over 300,000 widows in receipt of widow's pensions and widowed mother's allowances. The total number of widows drawing pensions is much larger because when a widow reaches 60 her widow's pension is automatically changed into a retirement pension, but until she reaches 65 the earnings rule continues to apply.

MATERNITY BENEFIT

Under the old Health Insurance Scheme maternity benefit usually consisted of a single grant, though many Approved Societies made second or additional grants. The National Insurance Act, influenced by international labour conventions about conditions of work for married women, introduced a new idea in the form of a special benefit called maternity allowance with the aim of making it easier for women to give up work well before the date on which they expected to be confined; it also provided an attendance allowance of £1 a week for four weeks following the birth of the child for women who did not qualify for the new maternity allowance.

Experience gained in the first few years working of these provisions suggested that they were not meeting the requirements of women in industry and the National Insurance Advisory Committee was asked to consider whether, without increasing the liability of the National Insurance Fund, changes could be made in the details of the scheme of maternity benefits which would enable the monetary needs of women in relation to maternity to be more adequately met.

The Committee's proposals, which, subject to modifications in rates of benefit, were embodied in an amending Act, made a number of changes in the earlier provisions for maternity benefits. One change was to differentiate between confinements taking place at home and those taking place in a maternity home or hospital making free provision under the National Health Service by paying a larger grant for the former. It was also found that the maternity allowance, which had been intended as a provision for the married woman who was in regular employment to which she intended to return within a reasonable time after the birth of her child, was to a large extent being paid to women who had no intention of continuing in employment after the arrival of the child. Changes were therefore made in the contribution conditions for the payment of this allowance with the object of limiting it to the group of women for whom it was originally intended. It is too early to say how far this object is being achieved.

D

DEATH GRANT

The only entirely new benefit provided by the 1946 Act was a grant payable on the death of an insured contributor or his wife or dependent child. For an adult the full grant is £25 but less may be paid in some cases as the benefit is one of those to which the principle of reducing benefit where the full amount of contributions required by the relevant contribution conditions has not been paid, has been applied. For a child the grant varies from £7 10s. for a child under 3 to £18 15s. for one between 6 and 17. The grant is intended to be for funeral and other expenses. It is usually payable to the person who meets the funeral expenses, but a person who has not paid for the funeral may receive it if he has incurred other expenses such as for mourning. Being a completely new benefit there are restrictions which exclude payment or reduce the amount in certain cases where, owing to the age of the person concerned, few or no contributions have been paid under the new scheme, or they have only been paid for a short period.

The benefit is administered by local offices in close co-operation with Registrars of Births, Deaths and Marriages and it is rare for any question about entitlement to arise. Any dispute between two or more people both of whom are *prima facie* entitled is decided by the Minister and not by the statutory authorities who normally decide claims to benefit.

In January, 1955, the Minister came to the conclusion that it was time to review the working of the death grant and referred it to the National Insurance Advisory Committee for advice. They found that in general it had worked satisfactorily and that most of the claims had been settled without any difficulty. They drew attention, however, to the rules which governed cases where the benefit was claimed by more than one person, under which a second payment of benefit sometimes had to be made to a late claimant with a better title than an earlier claimant to whom payment had already been made. They pointed out that it was rarely possible to recover the earlier payment as it usually had been received in perfect good faith and might indeed already have been spent. They were also concerned about the rule which prevented payment to a corporation such as the Public Trustee or a bank which was acting as executor under a will, or to a trade union which made itself responsible for the funeral expenses of one of its members in the absence of relatives. To meet these and several other similar cases the committee recommended that the rules governing the payment of the benefit should be altered so as to make it payable to the personal representative of the deceased or, failing him, to anyone who undertook to meet the funeral expenses; corporations and similar bodies were to be eligible under both heads. They also suggested certain relaxations of time limits for claiming the grant and the inclusion of certain children who had previously been excluded. The committee reported in December, 1956, and their recommendations have since been adopted.

GUARDIAN'S ALLOWANCE

As the death of the breadwinner may leave children unprovided for, the Act provides a special benefit for orphaned children in the shape of a weekly allowance payable to the person who takes the child into his family after the death of the parents. This allowance is not payable to an orphanage or similar institution. It continues to be paid so long as the child is under the age limit, which is the same as that laid down for the payment of family allowances. The benefit is unique in one respect since it is the only national insurance benefit for which there are no contribution conditions; all that is required is that one at least of the parents should have been insured under the scheme.

CHAPTER V

Industrial Injuries

*

GENERAL

THE scheme of compensation or benefit for industrial injuries embodied in the National Insurance (Industrial Injuries) Act, 1946, took the place of workmen's compensation for all accidents occurring after 5th July, 1948, but workmen's compensation continues to be paid to men injured before that date. The new scheme broke fresh ground: it brought what had been a matter between the man and his employer within the ambit of the social services administered by the State; and while continuing the principle of providing more benefit for industrial injuries and diseases than for other injuries or for ordinary illnesses, it proposed a new method of calculating compensation for such injuries. Many people have argued that while special provision for industrial injuries was right and indeed natural so long as it was provided by the employer in whose service the injury was sustained, the case for providing it under a comprehensive scheme of national insurance was far less obvious. But there never was any doubt that as men incapacitated by industrial injuries had for years received better terms than those suffering from ordinary sickness, special provision for industrial injuries would have to form part of the new social security plans.

The Beveridge Report contained suggestions for dealing with industrial injuries based on the fact that the effects of such injuries rarely last more than thirteen weeks. The proposal, in brief, was that short-term injuries should be dealt with under the new sickness benefit provisions of the main scheme and special benefits should only be provided for those whose industrial injuries persisted beyond thirteen weeks. From the administrative point of view this proposal had much to commend it as it would have considerably reduced the number of cases where it would be necessary to decide whether a particular injury was industrial or not, a question which had led to a great deal of litigation under workmen's compensation; but it suffered from the fatal defect that as the great majority of men suffering from industrial injuries would be dealt with under the ordinary sickness benefit scheme they would not get the preferential terms to which they had been accustomed under workmen's compensation.

A number of ideas were considered and ultimately a contributory scheme covering everyone working under a contract of service was adopted which embodied the principles of the war pensions scheme, under which pensions vary with the severity of the injury as assessed by a medical board. The analogy between men suffering from service injuries and from industrial injuries broke down on one vital point. The soldier who is injured remains in the Army until his injury has healed or at least until his condition has been so far stabilized as to enable some forecast of its future course to be made; in the meanwhile he receives his service pay and is generally cared for. Nothing corresponding to this was possible in a scheme for civilians. When a man is disabled by injury his wages usually cease and some form of benefit had to be provided which could be put into payment quickly and without waiting to see how serious the injury would turn out to be.

The industrial injuries scheme therefore provides two separate types of benefit. Subject to a limit of six months, what is known as injury benefit is payable during total incapacity due to an industrial accident; this is paid at a flat rate irrespective of the extent of the injury. If incapacity persists after total incapacity has ceased, or beyond six months from the date of the accident, disablement benefit is payable. This varies with the degree of injury as assessed by a medical board and usually takes the form of a pension for a fixed period or for life, though in minor cases a gratuity may be paid. A special allowance known as the unemployability supplement is payable to the man who is permanently unable to work as the result of his injury, and if his injury is so severe as to require regular attendance a further allowance, known as the constant attendance allowance, will also be paid.

Although injury benefit and the maximum rate of disablement benefit are both considerably in excess of sickness benefit under the main scheme, it was quickly realized that the new method of calculating the long-term benefit would mean that in certain cases a man might get less from the new scheme than he would have received from his employer by way of workmen's compensation. These are cases where a comparatively slight injury has a disproportionate effect on the man's earning power. Examples frequently quoted are an engine driver's eye or a compositor's finger. If an engine driver suffers even a slight injury to his sight he may lose his job and so may a compositor who injures his forefinger. To a medical board the injury to the eye or finger would seem very slight in comparison with an injury which resulted in a man being crippled for life and their assessment of the degree of disability would be correspondingly small. Under workmen's compensation, on the other hand, the injured man might well get compensation at the maximum rate allowed by the Act as he would lose most of his earning power. While the Bill was still before Parliament the simple scheme of disablement benefit based solely on the medical assessment of the degree of injury was modified by the introduction of an allowance, to which the name of 'special hardship allowance' was given. This allowance is payable in addition to the ordinary disablement benefit in cases where minor injuries prevent a man from resuming his old occupation, but the two together cannot exceed the maximum rate of benefit for total disablement. A list of the current rates of industrial injury benefits and allowances is given in Appendix III.

The Workmen's Compensation Acts covered not only injuries by accident but also certain diseases known as industrial diseases. It has always been more difficult to devise a reasonable scheme of compensation or benefit for industrial diseases than for industrial accidents. Injury by accident usually occurs at a definite time and place and, although there are bound to be marginal cases, it is usually a simple matter to decide whether a particular injury arose out of the man's work or not. The onset of disease and its origin in a particular case are far more difficult, and in many cases impossible, to determine. Medical science is still in doubt about the real causes of many common diseases and it would be mere guesswork to attempt to attribute the origin of such a disease in a particular case to something arising out of the man's work rather than to his general physical condition or to his general environment. This uncertainty about the origin of a disease creates a special problem in relation to proposals to award compensation for diseases claimed to be of industrial origin. Under workmen's compensation, where the liability rested on the employer, it would have been unreasonable to saddle a particular employer with liability for compensating a workman unless the disease could with reasonable certainty be attributed to the nature of the work on which he was employed. Under the industrial injuries scheme, where the liability rests not on a particular employer but on a common fund, this difficulty disappears but, as benefits for industrial injuries are much more favourable than sickness benefit under the main scheme, it is still necessary to distinguish between industrial and ordinary disease in order to decide whether industrial or ordinary rates of benefit are payable.

The method adopted for dealing with industrial diseases, both by the Workmen's Compensation Acts and by the new scheme, has been to concentrate on certain kinds of disease where medical science can point with reasonable certainty to the cause and identify it with something connected with the nature of the man's occupation, and to prescribe or schedule in regulations these diseases and the occupations which give rise to them. Where this is done, men in the prescribed occupations who suffer from the corresponding diseases can claim benefit in much the same way as for an injury due to an industrial accident. This method is flexible and from the administrative point of view it has worked well, but it has not satisfied those who think that industrial injury benefits should be payable in respect of any disease due to the nature of a man's occupation in just the same way as it is payable for any accident arising out of his work or, in exceptional cases, where the onset of a disease can in itself be regarded as an industrial accident.

The whole subject was exhaustively examined by a committee presided over by Mr. F. W. Beney, Q.C., whose report was published in 1955 (Cmd. 9548), and by a majority they recommended against any change in the method of dealing with compensation for industrial diseases. They pressed, however, for further efforts to be made to determine what diseases, in addition to those already prescribed, could be regarded as due to the nature of the work and should be added to the list.

As accidents which occurred before the Appointed Day for the introduction of the new scheme, and cases of disease contracted before that date, continue to be dealt with under the provisions of the Workmen's Compensation Acts, the two schemes will continue to exist side by side for many years to come. When the industrial injuries scheme was first announced it was contemplated that the old workmen's compensation cases would be taken over and transferred to the new benefit scheme, subject to suitable financial adjustments with the employers on whom the liability for workmen's compensation rested. Experience of the new scheme soon made it clear that to transfer the old cases to the new scheme would result in many men with slight injuries, who might be getting full workmen's compensation on the ground that they had lost most of their earning power, getting substantially less under the new scheme because they were suffering from injuries which, medically speaking, were relatively trivial. The proposal to transfer the old cases to the new scheme was accordingly abandoned, and attention given to the possibility of making further provision for those injured before the new Act came into operation. Details of several schemes which have been provided for special groups of old cases are given later on in this chapter and in Appendix IV. The preparation and execution of these schemes added considerably to the administrative difficulties which accompanied the introduction of the industrial injuries scheme.

ADMINISTRATION

Two points called for special thought in planning the administrative arrangements for the new industrial injuries scheme. It would be necessary to decide in each case whether the claimant's injury was an industrial injury or not and there would be a whole host of new medical questions for which special machinery would have to be set up.

The phrase used in the National Insurance (Industrial Injuries) Act to describe the kind of injury that would attract industrial injury benefits was 'personal injury . . . by accident arising out of and in the course of [a man's] employment'. This phrase was copied from the Workmen's Compensation Acts and in general the rules laid down by the Courts in workmen's compensation cases would have to be applied in interpreting it, though some of them were modified in a claimant's favour by the Act. It was a formidable business to set out to instruct a thousand local offices in the intricacies of a subject which had baffled so many learned judges. Considerable sums may be involved in a decision which may lead to a pension for life and once a local officer has decided that a particular accident is industrial that decision cannot be reviewed, except in cases of fraud. The idea of administering the Act through a limited number of specialized offices was considered but it was rejected in favour of the broad principle that to give the public the service it expected every local office would have to be able to deal with every kind of national insurance business. In actual practice there does not seem to have been much difficulty in reaching reasonable decisions on the preliminary question whether an injury was industrial. Most claims are straightforward and if the local insurance officer is in doubt he can refer to an expert at Regional Headquarters, or in an extreme case refrain from giving a decision himself and refer the case to the local appeal tribunal for decision. The machinery for deciding industrial injury questions (other than medical questions) is the same as for questions under the main scheme: the same local tribunals serve both services and the National Insurance Commissioner is also the National Insurance (Industrial Injuries) Commissioner, though there are some differences in procedure between the two schemes which are noted in Chapter VIII.

As the amount of a disability pension was to depend on a medical assessment of the degree of disablement, the machinery for deciding these medical questions was all-important. In many ways these questions would be similar to those with which the medical boards of the Ministry of Pensions had for years been accustomed to deal and it was at one time contemplated that the Ministry of Pensions would do all the medical boarding work under the new scheme as agents for the Ministry of National Insurance. When it came to the point, however, it was felt that it would be a mistake to appear to identify the new civilian scheme too closely with the administration of service pensions; there are, moreover, some important technical differences between the status of the medical boards under the two schemes. Under the Royal Warrant for war pensions the decision on the amount of a pension rests (subject to the right of appeal to the special tribunals described in Chapter III) with the Minister and the ordinary medical boards are advisory rather than adjudicatory bodies. Under the industrial injuries scheme the decision of a medical board is binding on the Minister subject to certain powers to refer a case to one of the medical appeal tribunals set up under the Act. It was, moreover, foreseen that many more boards would be required for the new scheme and that some of these would have to be located in places where they were not required for war pension purposes. It was accordingly decided that the Ministry of National Insurance should set up its own medical boards but that there should be close co-operation with the Ministry of Pensions over the selection of doctors to sit on the boards, and over the use of premises where the boards would sit. Since the amalgamation of the two Ministries co-operation has become still closer, but in the meantime the number of war pension cases has substantially diminished while the volume of industrial injuries work is steadily increasing.

There has been close co-operation between the Ministry and the British Medical Association in recruiting doctors to sit on medical boards. Most of these doctors are in ordinary practice and only in the case of the special boards that deal with claims arising out of the industrial diseases known as pneumoconiosis and byssinosis are they on the staff of the Ministry. The policy has been to bring in as many doctors in regular practice as possible rather than doctors who do nothing but sit on medical boards; both because it would increase the confidence of the claimants in the boards' decisions and also because it would help to interest general practitioners in industrial injuries and diseases. For the same reasons Hospital Boards were asked to provide accommodation for medical boards on hospital premises wherever possible.

The Act gives certain rights of appeal from the decision of a medical board to specially constituted medical appeal tribunals each consisting of a chairman and two medical practitioners. It was vital to provide medical appeal tribunals whose status and constitution would carry conviction, not only with the claimants whose cases they would decide, but also with the doctors serving on medical boards whose decisions they would have to review and might overrule. It was accordingly decided to ask the Lord Chancellor to nominate members of the Bar of the highest standing to act as chairmen of the new tribunals and for the medical members to consult the Presidents of the Royal Colleges in London and the Heads of the University Medical Schools elsewhere. In this way a series of tribunals has been established whose decisions have won general acceptance. There are fourteen of these tribunals and no machinery exists for co-ordinating their decisions. This has not led to as much difficulty as might have been expected because almost all the decisions deal with the physical condition of a particular claimant and they are often arrived at after the injured man has been examined by the medical members of the tribunal. It is rarely, therefore, that any opportunity of comparing decisions of one tribunal with those of another offers itself. If a tribunal makes an error of law in arriving at its decision, for example, on a point concerning the interpretation of regulations affecting the assessment of injuries, an application can be made to the Courts to have the decision set aside. The possibility of issuing notes of leading decisions by medical appeal tribunals was discussed with the chairmen of the tribunals shortly after the Act came into operation, but it was generally felt that the cases they would have to deal with did not lend themselves to reporting in this way and it was decided not to attempt it.

SPECIAL HARDSHIP ALLOWANCE

Reference has already been made to the reasons which led to the introduction of the special hardship allowance for men prevented by their injuries from resuming their old occupations. In its original form this allowance was only payable where the man was found to be incapable, and likely to remain permanently incapable, of following his regular occupation, and of earning as much in some other occupation as he was accustomed to earn before his accident. It was soon realized that with modern methods of treatment and rehabilitation some time would in many cases elapse before a doctor would be prepared to say what permanent effect an injury was likely to have on a man's ability to earn his living and in the meantime the injured man would get no special allowance. Moreover, closer comparison between medical assessments in certain types of injury and the corresponding payments under the workmen's compensation scheme showed that the amount originally fixed for the special hardship allowance (11s. 3d. a week) was too low if the new scheme was to stand comparison with the old. A special Act was accordingly passed in 1948 making the amount depend on the loss of earnings sustained with a maximum of 20s. (since raised to 34s.) and making the allowance payable while the effects of the injury were still temporary.

This change in the conditions of the allowance completely altered its character. In its original form it was expected to be a permanent allowance payable in a comparatively small number of cases. In its new form it is payable in a large number of cases and often for short periods and it has become one of the major preoccupations in the administration of the Industrial Injuries Act. In his first quinquennial review of the working of the Act the Government Actuary pointed out that about one-half of the total number of disablement pensioners were receiving special hardship allowance and that the average amount of the allowance was appreciably larger than the average disablement pension.

In terms of administration this has meant the reintroduction of much of the flavour of workmen's compensation which it was the intention of the new scheme to remove. Most injured men are able to get back to work of some kind once their injury has healed, but many of them have to accept work other than that which they were doing before they were injured. They may, therefore, be entitled to special hardship allowance, and to decide whether it is payable to a particular individual it is necessary to compare the wages he was earning before his accident with his present earning power. This comparison between pre- and post-accident earnings was fundamental to the old workmen's compensation scheme and gave rise to many difficulties from which it was hoped to escape under the new scheme. Moreover, since, as the Government Actuary has pointed out, the average rate of special hardship allowance is larger than the average rate of disablement pension, medical assessments which were originally intended to govern the rate at which disablement benefit under the industrial injuries scheme would be paid, tend to be pushed into the background in many cases, and the all-important factor in deciding how much benefit is to be paid becomes once more the comparison between pre- and post-accident earnings. It is too soon to measure the long-term effects of this change in the character of the scheme, but it has certainly added to the difficulties of officers who have to decide claims to benefit and who, as the result of the introduction of the allowance, have to consider complicated questions connected with wage rates and earning capacity as well as distinguishing between different jobs, often within the same industry, in order to decide whether a man has resumed his regular occupation or not.

INDUSTRIAL DISEASES

In general the administration of the provisions of the Act relating to industrial diseases has not given rise to much difficulty. The list of diseases covered by the new scheme when it was first introduced included all those provided for under the workmen's compensation scheme and further diseases have since been added. Where there is doubt whether some new disease should be added to the list the advice of a special Committee of the Industrial Injuries Advisory Council may be sought and two of the five additions so far made have resulted from enquiries undertaken by this Committee. The most striking addition to the list, because it was the first instance when a communicable disease which was common among the general public was added to the list, was the addition in 1951 of tuberculosis for certain nurses and others specially exposed to infection. The criteria governing the selection of diseases for addition to the list are laid down in the Act and they were examined and explained by a committee under the chairmanship of His Honour Judge Dale which reported in 1948 (Cmd. 7557).

One group of diseases has occupied such an important place in the administration of the Act as to require special mention. This is the group of diseases known as pneumoconiosis and byssinosis which are caused by working in dusty surroundings. From the point of view of providing compensation or benefit these diseases have the special features that they cannot be cured and that a man suffering from them may live for many years and may gradually get worse. Any award of benefit is therefore likely to be for a long period and will have to be reviewed from time to time.

A number of special schemes were made under the Workmen's Compensation Acts providing compensation for different types of these 'dust' diseases in different industries. In 1943 a scheme was made for the coal industry dealing in terms with pneumoconiosis. Although coal mining is the industry mainly affected, there were also schemes for other industries: byssinosis, for example, is a form of dust disease found among workers employed in certain processes in the cotton industry.

All these schemes made provision for special boards composed of doctors in the employ of the Home Office to diagnose the disease on a claim to compensation and to decide how far a man was disabled by it. These special boards were considered to be necessary because the diseases are difficult to detect in individual cases and the work called for special skill and knowledge not readily available among ordinary practitioners. These special medical boards won the confidence of the workers in the industries affected by the diseases and they were continued when the new scheme came into operation, the doctors being transferred to the new Ministry. The difficulty of their work was increased by the introduction of the concept of degrees of disablement. Under workmen's compensation it is only necessary to decide whether a man is suffering from the disease to an extent which makes it dangerous for him to continue at work and whether any resulting disablement should be regarded as total or partial. Under the new Act the board have to assess the degree of disability in percentage terms in the same way as other medical boards do for injuries caused by accident. The boards are independent bodies and it was essential to preserve their independence: at the same time a reasonable degree of uniformity in their assessments was necessary if dissatisfaction was to be avoided. It has called for long and patient work on the part of the Ministry's medical staff to secure this.

Another important change was made when the new scheme was introduced. Under workmen's compensation a coal miner found to be suffering from pneumoconiosis was 'suspended', which in effect meant that he could no longer be employed in coal mining. As the result of much patient research into the causes of the disease and into methods of removing or reducing its chief cause—dust—it was felt possible to discontinue the automatic suspension of men suffering from the disease and to put in its place a careful consideration of the claimant's condition with a view to advising him whether it was safe for him to continue working underground in specially approved conditions. The duty of giving this advice was given to the special medical boards and the new arrangements have resulted in a considerable number of men who would otherwise have been lost to the industry continuing at work as coal miners.

All the processes covered by the pneumoconiosis schemes made under the Workmen's Compensation Acts were included within the scope of the new Act and other processes have been added from time to time. In 1954, as the result of a long enquiry by the Industrial Injuries Advisory Council, the extent of insurance cover was extended to include anyone who contracted pneumoconiosis, which by this time doctors were prepared to say was exclusively an industrial disease that could only be caused by the conditions under which a man worked.

How large a part claims based on these dust diseases play in the administration of the industrial diseases provisions of the Act is made clear by the fact that in 1955 there were approximately 33,000 awards of benefit current in respect of them as compared with 7,000 awards for all other forms of industrial disease.

OLD WORKMEN'S COMPENSATION CASES

On 5th July, 1948, men injured by industrial accidents or diseases were divided into two classes. Those injured before that date continued to be dealt with under workmen's compensation, though they were given the benefit of some of the special allowances provided by the new Act; those injured after that date came under the new industrial injuries scheme. Various attempts were made to wind up the workmen's compensation scheme altogether. These having failed for reasons already explained, the position of several groups of men who for one reason or another were not getting workmen's compensation or were not getting the full benefits of that scheme attracted increasing attention. One such group consisted of men injured before 1924 who were not given retrospectively the benefit of increased rates of workmen's compensation introduced by the Act of 1943 nor the advantage of earlier amending legislation regarding the method of calculating compensation. In addition there were men suffering from pneumoconiosis and other diseases who, because they left an industry before the disease was made compensatable for that industry, or because they had not claimed within the time limits provided by the special schemes, were not in receipt of compensation at all.

It was not possible to put further liabilities retrospectively on employers who had had no opportunity of providing for them and it was realized from the outset that any provision that might be made for these men would have to come out of the Industrial Injuries Fund. The totally different bases of the workmen's compensation and industrial injuries schemes made it difficult to devise special schemes which would make adequate provision for these men without giving them better terms than those provided by either of the existing schemes for comparable cases.

Three special schemes have now been made. The first deals with men injured before 1924. As these men were entitled to some compensation the necessary data about pre-accident wages and conditions existed and it was therefore possible to devise a scheme for them the general effect of which was to put them, as from an Appointed Day, in broadly the same position as if the provisions of the later Workmen's Compensation Acts were then applied to them.

The pneumoconiosis cases were more difficult to deal with because they had never been given workmen's compensation and no records of their pre-accident employment wages existed. It was therefore felt to be impossible to deal with them in accordance with workmen's compensation principles. The scheme for these men provided two flat rates of benefit, a distinction being made only between the totally disabled and the partially disabled: for totally disabled men the rate was 40s. and for partially disabled men it was 20s. a week. In addition death benefits of sums up to £300 were provided for the dependants of people dying from the diseases. A similar scheme was made in 1954 for people suffering from skin cancer or excessive exposure to X-rays or radio-active substances.

With the gradual rise in the level in prices and the resulting increase in benefits under the new scheme increasing attention was directed to the position of the very considerable number of men on workmen's compensation who had received no increase in the basic amount of their compensation since the current maximum rates were fixed in 1943 except in so far as they qualified for the special allowances provided for serious cases under the new scheme. Where an injured man was working he benefited from the general rise in the level of wages, but the incomes of men in receipt of compensation at the maximum rate for total incapacity remained at the level fixed in 1943. Many discussions took place with the T.U.C. about these men and it was ultimately decided to provide a special allowance of 17s. 6d. a week for totally disabled men entitled to compensation or similar payments. This was provided by the Workmen's Compensation and Benefit (Supplementation) Act, 1956, and brought into operation in that year.

The last-mentioned Act is administered in the ordinary way by the ministry's local offices, but for the purpose of administering the three special schemes a Board was set up consisting of representatives of both sides of industry and of the Ministry under the chairmanship of an eminent lawyer who was also chairman of one of the medical appeal tribunals. Claims to benefit under the three schemes are decided by this Board and the machinery of the Ministry is available to provide medical advice where necessary; awards are paid by the Ministry in the ordinary way. This method of administration has undoubtedly been a success. The Board has had to deal with many awkward questions which were frequently made all the more difficult by lack of adequate information about the circumstances and conditions of the claimant at the time he first sustained the injury or contracted the disease many years ago. There has been little or no complaint about the way in which these questions have been handled and it may be doubted whether things would have gone so smoothly if the scheme had been administered by the Department in the ordinary way. Details of the various schemes and the numbers dealt with are given in Appendix IV.

CHAPTER VI

Family Allowances

*

GENERAL

THE family allowances scheme is the simplest to administer of all the schemes run by the Ministry. It would have been even simpler but for the decision to limit the allowances to families with two or more children. Families with only one child were excluded because family allowances had their origin in a desire to do something to relieve the hardship of low wage-earners with large families and it was reasonable to assume that one child could be supported out of the family earnings; but the decision undoubtedly made the scheme more complicated. If an allowance had been payable for every child in a family the allowances would have been children's allowances and could have been, as it were, attached to the child and allowed to follow him wherever he went. It was the introduction of the idea of the family of two or more children as the basis of the scheme which changed it from a scheme of children's allowances to one of family allowances; the family becomes all-important and its composition has to be carefully noted. In a family drawing an allowance there will always be one child below the prescribed age who does not himself attract an allowance but whose departure from the family or attainment of the school-leaving age may reduce or put an end to any allowance the family may be drawing. To understand the family allowance scheme it is important to remember that a person over the age of 18, or one who after leaving school is working but is not an apprentice, does not count as a child at all and that there will always be one less allowance in payment to a family than there are children below the prescribed age.

Further administrative complications were introduced when it was decided that instead of stopping an allowance on a child's fifteenth birthday (15 being the ordinary school-leaving age) it was to go on until the 1st August after his sixteenth (now until his eighteenth) birthday, if he continued in the meantime to receive full-time education or became an apprentice. When the Act was passed it was contemplated that the school-leaving age would be raised to 16 and if that had happened there would have been no difficulty; the choice of the 1st August following the sixteenth birthday as the final date would simply have meant that the allowance would continue while the child finished out the school year. Because the school-leaving age has remained at 15 a whole series of questions have been opened up about the circumstances in which a child who has left school can be regarded as continuing to receive full-time education or instruction or as serving as an apprentice. The introduction, in 1956, of a higher rate for third and subsequent children has also added to the complications of the scheme.

Most of the difficulties in administering family allowances relate either to the circumstances in which a child who is not living with its parents can be regarded as a member of their family or to the question whether a child who has left school and gone into some job for which it is receiving wages can be regarded as an apprentice.

A child living with its parents will be treated as a member of their family. If the child is living elsewhere it will only be treated as a member of its parents' family if they are maintaining it; an expression which is explained in the Family Allowances Act as meaning contributing at least 8s. a week towards its upkeep. Where the parents are separated special rules apply and it often becomes a difficult question to decide to which 'family' a child should be regarded as belonging.

As a parent will be regarded as maintaining a child that is not living with him if he sends it cash or clothes or other goods to the value of 8s. a week, it may well happen that the parent will continue to be entitled to draw an allowance in respect of a child who is for all practical purposes living with and being maintained by someone else. Allowances are not payable to the managers of children's homes nor to a Local Authority who has children in an institution or boarded out. A foster parent, however, may be able to claim provided the parent is not contributing towards the child's keep. There are special rules about children in approved schools, children committed by the Courts to the care of a Local Authority and children over whom a Local Authority has assumed parental rights; in general no allowance can be claimed for such a child even where the parent is contributing towards its keep. There are also special rules about the children of parents living abroad. In the ordinary way an allowance is not payable unless at least one parent is in the United Kingdom, but there are special rules for merchant seamen and members of the forces serving overseas. The child in respect of whom an allowance is claimed must also be living in this country, though for periods during which it is attending school abroad it is treated as though it were in this country. Where a family returns to the United Kingdom after residing abroad, a period of six months must elapse before an allowance can be claimed.

E

The vast majority of the allowances are payable to ordinary families with children living at home whose claims to an allowance give rise to no difficulty, but the number of marginal cases is sufficiently large and the problems they create sufficiently difficult to have led the Ministry to the view that it was better to administer family allowances centrally from Newcastle rather than to decentralize them to the local offices. The centralized system of appeals to Referees instead of to the local tribunals described in Chapter VIII also weighs against the administration of the scheme through local offices.

Although the administration is centred on Newcastle, claims are made at local offices and these offices will also carry out any local enquiries needed to clear up doubtful points. A claim to an allowance must be made by the mother unless the marriage has been broken by divorce or permanent separation, when special rules apply. The mother claims because, when the Bill was going through Parliament, an amendment was made declaring that the allowance belonged to her. Forms of claim are available at Post Offices as well as local offices and when completed can be handed in at a local office or posted to Newcastle. The mother is also asked, when making her claim, to fill in index slips giving particulars of the child. These slips form the basis of the family allowances index at Newcastle which contains particulars of the $8\frac{1}{2}$ million children included in families drawing allowances.

Unless some special point arises on a claim, the process of awarding an allowance is little more than a formality; it is simply a question of checking ages and the number of children in the family. About a quarter of a million initial claims are received every year; which of course means the birth of a second child in over a quarter of a million families. Nearly as many claims are received from families already receiving an allowance in respect of the birth of another child. There are about 15,000 children included in the families of persons other than their parents and there are also about 31,000 children not living with their parents who are included in their parents' families because the parents are contributing towards their upkeep.

When a child in a family which is drawing an allowance approaches 15 it becomes necessary to find out what he is going to do. In many cases the child will continue to attend regularly at school and there will be no difficulty in deciding that he can continue to be regarded as a child for family allowance purposes. Sometimes the child will leave school and become a trainee or he may take an ordinary job where he learns as he goes along. Marginal cases of this kind are common. If the child, to use the language of the Act, is 'in receipt of earnings which provide him, wholly or substantially, with a livelihood' he cannot be regarded as an apprentice. If the wages the child is getting do not rule him out it may be necessary to find out exactly what training he is receiving. As the result of some years of administering the Act, the Newcastle office has collected a large amount of information about the conditions under which young entrants to industry work: they range from formal apprenticeship to something more resembling the Dotheboys Hall system of education based on a severely practical method of learning on the job. Under the Act as originally passed a child who had attained the school-leaving age of 15 could not be counted as a child for family allowance purposes unless he was actually receiving full-time education or serving as an apprentice. It was represented that this provision operated unfairly in the case of children who owing to some physical or mental handicap were unable to attend school or to go out to work, and it was urged that these children should automatically continue to be counted for allowance purposes until they reach 16 at which age they are entitled to receive National Assistance in their own right. Under the National Insurance and Family Allowances Act, 1956, invalid and disabled children are now automatically included for family allowance purposes up to the age of 16.

Nearly two-thirds of the 3¼ million or so families drawing family allowances in 1956 were drawing one allowance of 8s. a week, which means that they have two children under the prescribed age in their family; 90 per cent. of them have not more than three children. What constitutes a 'large' family in these days may be a matter of opinion, but figures like these do at least show how far matters have travelled since Miss Rathbone and others pressed for family allowances as a means of preventing hardship to low wage-earners with large families; there are no income limits to restrict the allowance to 'low' wage-earners. The scheme as it stands costs about £110 million a year and as there are no insurance contributions the whole of this is provided by the Exchequer. It would more than double the cost to pay an allowance in respect of first and only children in a family, and it is not easy to understand the point of view of those who, like the Royal Commission on Population, have advocated this step.

ADMINISTRATION

About 1,000 people are engaged on the administration of family allowances at Newcastle. Their main tasks are to decide initial claims; to adjust existing allowances to meet changes of circumstances such as additions to the family, the death of a child or the attainment of the age limit by a child included in the calculation of the allowance (it is estimated that about half a million such adjustments are made every year); to prepare, issue and renew order books for families to whom allowances have been awarded and to maintain the family allowance index. Various suggestions for simplifying the scheme with the idea of economizing in the administration have been made from time to time but, as it is unlikely that any simplification which deprived people of rights they already possessed would meet with general approval, these ideas are usually found on examination to cost a good deal more than they would save. The cost of administration cannot be regarded as unduly high; in 1956 £2¼ million was spent on administration and £114 million on allowances.

Family allowances are paid by means of books of orders which can be cashed at a Post Office selected by the applicant. The books generally run for a year but shorter books are issued when it is clear that the amount payable will cease before the end of that period. Although the allowance belongs to the mother either parent, in the ordinary case, can cash the orders.

The work at Newcastle is organized as a self-contained unit (colloquially known as 'FAM') with its own index and records and its own machinery for preparing and issuing the allowance books. Proposals have been made to amalgamate the 'FAM' index with the general index of national insurance contributors in which many of the same names appear. It was, however, found on examination that the resulting index would be so unwieldy that, far from bringing about any economy, it would add substantially to the time taken to consult it and thus to the cost of the staff employed. Various methods of arranging family allowances work have been tried, though the preparation and issue of order books has always been separate from the work of awarding and revising allowances. Originally the awarding work was organized more or less on the 'conveyor belt' system with special sections dealing with problems like whether a child over 15 could continue to be included in an allowance on the ground that he was receiving full-time instruction, but the group system with about one hundred self-contained groups each consisting of six officers seems to give the best results though some specialist sections have been retained. Family allowances were the first of the new schemes to be brought into operation and there were some anxious moments when, within a month of the announcement that the Ministry was ready to receive claims, over 1,400,000 were received, a figure which four months later had grown to over

$2\frac{1}{4}$ million; it was originally estimated that there might be as many as $2\frac{1}{2}$ million claims.

It was always intended that the family allowances administration should be housed in the Ministry's new offices to be built at Newcastle, but work on these offices only started in 1946 and when it was decided to bring the family allowances scheme into force in August of that year and to start receiving applications at the end of March, two years before the main scheme started, temporary accommodation had to be found. It was in these circumstances that FAM started operations in the spring of 1946 in a factory on the Team Valley Estate where it remained until October, 1946, when, with the work of launching the new scheme safely behind them, the administration moved to Newcastle and took over the first block of the new offices. The transfer of 2,500 staff with all its furniture and equipment, including the records of $2\frac{1}{2}$ million claims and large batteries of office machinery, took four days.

Despite the handicap of improvised premises and the novelty of the work, the original claims were all dealt with in good time and there were few complaints of delay. In most cases an allowance was granted and only about 2 or 3 per cent. of the claims were rejected; many of these were claims made under a misunderstanding of the nature of the scheme as the claimant only had one child below the prescribed age.

The proportion of initial claims rejected has steadily fallen as the scheme has become better understood and today it is comparatively rare for a claim to be made in circumstances where an allowance is not payable.

CHAPTER VII

Finance and Insured Contributors

*

FINANCE plays a large part in the work of the Ministry and its financial problems are complicated by the fact that part of the cost of the services it administers is met from insurance contributions paid into the National Insurance and Industrial Injuries Funds and part from moneys voted annually by Parliament.

THE VOTES

War pensions and family allowances are paid out of voted moneys and the usual process of preparing estimates has to be gone through each year for these services. Estimating for war pensions is fairly straightforward as the number of pensioners is known and in the absence of major military operations is not likely to increase. The preparation of the estimate for family allowances involves some rather complicated calculations. As a family allowance is only paid to a family which has two or more children below the school-leaving age or still at school the number of allowances which will be paid in any year does not depend on the total number of children born or leaving school in the year but on the number born into families which already have at least one child and the number leaving school in families with two or more children. To arrive at this figure a careful examination of the birth statistics over a number of years is necessary. The final out-turn of the estimate in any year is complicated by the widespread habit of saving up allowances for several weeks and spending them in one lump sum. One week's allowances represents about £2 million so that it does not take much in the way of a change from saving them up to spending them to turn a prospective surplus into a deficit. For this reason the incidence of Easter is important in deciding whether the money in hand towards the end of the financial year will prove sufficient or whether a supplementary estimate must be sought. If Easter falls within the current financial year many more orders will be cashed than if it falls outside. There have been some anxious moments for the Accounting Officer and his advisers and in some years the out-turn of the account has been very close, the estimates being within £150,000 of the amount spent on a total of over £100 million.

Annual estimates are also required to cover the cost of the Ministry's administration as a whole. This is paid in the first instance out of voted moneys, though most of it is eventually recovered from the two Insurance Funds. The preparation of this estimate follows the normal course, but the total cost of administration has to be divided in due proportion between the Vote Services and the Fund Services and then the amount falling in the latter has to be split between the two funds. Fixed proportions based on cost surveys are used for this purpose. In the same way, insurance contributions for the employed class which are paid in the form of a combined contribution for both schemes, have to be divided between the two schemes on the basis of information provided by the Government Actuary. The special contribution towards the National Health Service, formerly 10d. a week for men, and doubled by the National Health Service Contributions Act of 1957, also has to be separated out and accounted for to the Health Departments.

THE FUNDS

The financial arrangements for the National Insurance and the Industrial Injury Funds do not follow the normal lines of Government Finance; they are not covered by the usual procedure of Estimates, Votes, Appropriations-in-Aid and Appropriation Accounts. The income of the two funds, which is derived from contributions paid by insured contributors and their employers and from Exchequer Supplements, together with the interest earned by the invested funds, is paid into the two separate funds as it becomes available and no estimate of the expected revenue is prepared for presentation to Parliament. An estimate is, however, presented to Parliament to cover the Exchequer contribution, which, in the case of national insurance, is about one-sixth of the sum contributed by the other two parties for the employed class and one-third for the self-employed and non-employed, and, in the case of industrial injuries, one-fifth.

Sums due for pensions and benefits are similarly payable directly out of the funds and no estimate is prepared for presentation to Parliament of the expected outgoings during the year. The Government Actuary does, however, prepare annual reports on each of the funds which are presented to Parliament by the Treasury and these give in considerable detail an account of the financial position of the two schemes.

Most of the money paid out in pensions and benefits (other than unemployment benefit) is paid in cash over the counter by Post Offices and the Post Office has to be kept in funds to meet the demands made on it. On the other hand, by far the greater part of the money paid in contributions is taken by the Post Office in payment for national insurance stamps and the Post Office has to account for this to the Ministry. Among the processes included in this system of cross-accounting between the Ministry and the General Post Office is one of checking the postal drafts cashed by the Post Office for benefits such as sickness benefits, against the amounts originally authorized by the local office of the Ministry. This process has been found to be necessary, partly as a step in determining the amount due to the General Post Office, partly to detect frauds through alterations in postal drafts and also to trace drafts that claimants say they have not received. The process is highly mechanized but as something like 50 million drafts are issued every year the task of checking them is a formidable one.

The Fund Accounts are audited by the Comptroller and Auditor-General and come before the Public Accounts Committee in the ordinary way; the sums involved are indeed so large that the Committee has made a practice of summoning the Permanent Secretary as the Accounting Officer of the Department to give oral evidence every year.

THE GOVERNMENT ACTUARY'S REPORTS

The National Insurance Act and the Industrial Injuries Act require the Government Actuary to make yearly reports to the Treasury on the finances of the respective schemes; these reports are laid before Parliament.

In these reports the Government Actuary examines in great detail the state of the funds, the income from contributions and interest and the outgoings in the shape of benefits and pensions. Every five years he makes a full actuarial review of each of the schemes which is also published. Students of these extremely complicated financial problems are recommended to study these reports, but the following brief account of the financial basis of the two funds may be of interest to the more general reader.

THE FINANCIAL BASIS OF THE FUNDS

Although the main scheme and the industrial injuries scheme are both insurance schemes they were designed to meet very different contingencies and this difference is reflected in their financial structure.

When the National Insurance Fund and the National Insurance

(Reserve) Fund were formed in 1948 they took over the balances belonging to the National Health Insurance Fund, the Contributory Pensions Scheme and also the old Unemployment Fund which, after years of insolvency, had accumulated large balances during the war when there was practically no unemployment. The two new funds started with a balance of about £900 million, of which £546 million represented the balance of the Unemployment Fund. On the 5th July, 1948, the old funds ceased to have any separate existence; since then all national insurance contributions and payments have been paid into and made out of one fund, the National Insurance Fund. The existence of the large balances which the Insurance Fund and the Reserve Fund inherited has tended to obscure what is really happening to the finances of the scheme.

The weekly contribution payable jointly by insured persons, employer and Exchequer is based on actuarial calculations, but the scheme is not 'funded' in the sense in which this term is usually understood in connection with superannuation schemes. The contributions are related to persons entering the scheme at the age of 16, and the assumption underlying the calculation is that the contributions would be allowed to accumulate at interest in the fund except in so far as they were required to pay benefits to which the contributors became entitled. This does not in fact happen, as the contributions are used to meet claims to benefits by older beneficiaries and contributors who, in the nature of things, have not been paying contributions throughout their working lives at the rates appropriate for current benefits. The only fund which is being built up to meet the liabilities of the scheme that will emerge in the form of an excess of expenditure over income as the number of pensioners grows, thus consists of the assets taken over from the former schemes, and the surplus of income over expenditure in the early years of the scheme. It was never intended that this should be sufficient to meet the liability for pensions not covered by contributions, and indeed the surplus income in the early years of the fund was quite fortuitous and was mainly due to the negligible amount of unemployment in those years. The balance is underwritten by the Exchequer, which will have to make good the deficiency as and when it emerges by way of annual lump sum grants. Current legislation provides for such grants, not exceeding £325 million in total, for the five-year period 1955–60 and thereafter such sums as Parliament may determine.

In calculating the weekly contributions, the amount of sickness likely to rank for benefit and the number of pensioners and how long they were likely to survive to draw their pensions were matters which the Government Actuary could estimate. The position was very different in relation to unemployment. In 1944 the country had adopted the policy of full employment and there was no means of foreseeing how much unemployment there would be. To calculate the cost of unemployment benefit, which was an essential element in working out the proper contribution, the Government Actuary had to use assumptions given to him by the Government of the day as to the average level of unemployment. Originally an assumed average of $8\frac{1}{2}$ per cent. unemployment was adopted as a probably safe basis for financial purposes, but in the light of experience the basis was altered to 4 per cent. in 1951; in fact, unemployment has been well below even the latter figure. The increase in the funds during the years immediately following the inception of the scheme (and to a lesser extent subsequently) was largely due to the low level of unemployment compared with the figure taken as the basis for calculating the contribution—between 1948 and 1956 the balances in the funds increased by about £600 million.

Most of the problems connected with the National Insurance Funds arise from what has been done in regard to pensions. When pensions were raised from 10s. to 26s. in 1946 and on every subsequent occasion when they have been raised, existing pensioners and those coming up for pension subsequently were given the higher rate of pension although they had never paid the contribution appropriate to that rate of pension, or would only pay it for a short period. The Government Actuary has estimated that in 1953, people then drawing pensions had only paid about 5 per cent. of the value of the pensions granted to them. This uncovered liability for pensions of the growing number of pensioners is the main reason for the steadily increasing payments which the Exchequer will have to make to the fund to maintain its solvency.

The financial implications of the increasing cost of pensions are discussed at length in the report of a Committee set up in 1953 to study the economic and financial problems of the provisions for old age. The Report was published in 1954 (Cmd. 9333) and to it the reader is referred if he desires more detailed information on what is undoubtedly the main problem confronting the finances of the national insurance scheme.

THE INVESTED FUNDS

At the end of the financial year 1955–6 the National Insurance Fund had a balance of £318 million and the Reserve Fund a balance of £1,167 million. The National Insurance Fund is the current account into which contribution income is paid together with the interest earned by both the funds and out of it sums required for pensions, benefits and administration are paid. The Reserve Fund forms a standing reserve only to be drawn on in very exceptional circumstances. Transfers may be made at any time from the National Insurance Fund to the Reserve Fund by the Ministry with Treasury approval and £300 million was transferred in 1952 and a further £100 million in 1955. Payments out of the Reserve Fund can only be made on the authority of a resolution of the House of Commons.

The National Insurance Act placed these funds under the control and management of the Minister, but it also provided that surplus moneys belonging to the funds were to be paid over to the National Debt Commissioners and 'by them invested' in accordance with such directions as might be given by the Treasury, in securities authorized as investments for Savings Bank funds. The exact implications of these provisions were considered by the Public Accounts Committee and it was accepted that while it was for the Minister, as the person in control of the fund, to say what calls might be expected to be made on the fund year by year for payments of pensions, benefits, and administration, the responsibility for selecting the best investments to meet these requirements rested, in the absence of any directions from the Treasury, on the National Debt Commissioners.

INDUSTRIAL INJURIES

The position of the Industrial Injuries Fund is very different. The Industrial Injuries Scheme was completely new; it took over no existing funds and inherited no liabilities towards existing beneficiaries. From the nature of the benefits provided it was to be expected that the full weight of the short-term 'industrial injury benefit' would be felt almost immediately, but that it would be many years before the cost of the long-term disability pensions reached its maximum. It was estimated that the fund would take between 30 and 40 years to reach maturity and in the meantime the cost of the scheme would go on increasing year by year, quite apart from any increase in rates of benefit. By maturity is meant the point at which the cost of new disability pensions would be balanced by the cessation, through death or other causes, of pensions already granted.

Such a scheme might have been financed on the 'assessment' basis; that is to say, the contribution charged at the outset might have been no more than was needed to cover the cost for a short period, say the first five years. The scheme would then have had to be reviewed every five years and the contribution adjusted to meet the estimated cost during the next quinquennium and so on. This would have meant that during the early years of the scheme, when the cost would be increasing year by year, contributions would have had to be raised every five years without any corresponding increase in benefits. This was felt to be too difficult to explain and on many grounds undesirable. The scheme was accordingly financed on the alternative plan of fixing contributions at rates which, apart from increases in benefit rates, could be maintained unchanged throughout. In the early years this would produce a surplus of income over outgoings which would be invested and it was calculated that the interest on the investments, together with receipts from contributions, would be sufficient to meet all demands on the fund when the cost of benefits reached its highest point.

The introduction of the special hardship allowance described in Chapter V considerably affected the position, as neither when it was first introduced nor when it was liberalized and increased in 1948 was any addition made to the contribution to cover the cost. In its original form it was very restricted and it was not expected to cost very much, but it now accounts for about one-third of the whole cost of disablement benefit, of which it forms part. Other charges have also been placed on the fund in the shape of the benefits under the special schemes also described in Chapter V. As a result the Government Actuary felt bound to point out in his First quinquennial review that the current contribution was insufficient to meet the eventual liabilities. He also pointed out that the estimates on which his forecast was based inevitably contain a considerable element of conjecture, especially as regards the future cost of the most important element, disablement benefit. It is therefore too early to say how matters will eventually turn out, though it is clear that for many years to come the Industrial Injuries fund will continue to grow, assuming there are no further changes in rates of benefit or that, if changes are made, they are covered by appropriate increases in the contributions. One of the difficulties in adjusting the contribution under this scheme so as to produce the exact income required is that owing to the large number of contributors (over 20 million) an increase in the joint contribution of as little as one penny brings in an extra £4 million a year which represents about 11 per cent. of the present total outgoings on benefits and administration, and many of the extra charges which have at various times been placed on the fund did not by themselves involve the expenditure of anything like this sum, though taken together their incidence on the fund is substantial.

INSURED CONTRIBUTORS

About 21½ million people are liable to pay contributions under the National Insurance Scheme of whom about 16 million are men, 1½ million are married women who have chosen to be insured and

4 million single women. They are divided for insurance purposes into three classes who pay different rates of contribution and are entitled to different kinds (but not different rates) of benefits. The main class (Class I) comprises all people employed 'under a contract of service', the ordinary worker who works for an employer, of whom there are about 19½ million; persons in this class can qualify for all the benefits provided by the scheme. Class II consists of the self-employed person, who earns his living by working on his own account like the small shopkeeper, the author and most professional men; there are about 1½ million of these and they are entitled to all the benefits under the main scheme except unemployment benefit. The third class is the non-employed contributor, the person who for some reason or another does not, at any rate for the time being, have to work for a living. There are only about half a million of them at any one time but they include a number of people like students who will soon pass into Class I or Class II.

Under previous schemes only those now in Class I were compulsorily insurable and not all of them as there were many exceptions and exemptions including a general income limit which barred non-manual workers who earned more than £250 a year (raised in 1942 to £420). The modern plan is universal and everyone must, unless excepted, be insured though they may pass from one class to another as their circumstances alter. The most important exceptions are married women who, even if they are working, can elect not to pay contributions, and self-employed or non-employed people with incomes of less than £156 a year who can claim to be exempted on the ground that they cannot afford to be insured. This widening of the scope of insurance has changed the character of the task of deciding questions of insurability. Previously it was a question of whether a person was insurable or not and many otherwise difficult cases were ruled out automatically by the income limit; nowadays it is necessary to decide everyone's status for insurance purposes. Contributors who pass from one class to another as they become employed or start up on their own must also be allowed to retain the value of contributions paid in their previous class, but as it would obviously not be fair to allow a self-employed person who becomes employed in Class I to qualify for unemployment benefit solely on the strength of his Class II contributions, elaborate rules have had to be devised governing the circumstances in which, and how far, contributions paid in one class may be counted for benefit purposes in another class.

These questions, as well as the prior question of which class a contributor should be regarded as being in for insurance purposes, are decided by the Minister subject to an appeal on points of law to the High Court. Some of these cases are very complicated, especially on the borderline between the person who works under a contract of service and the person who undertakes to do certain work for another under a contract for services. A description of the way in which they are decided is given in Chapter VIII.

Under the industrial injuries scheme there is only one class; that of the ordinary worker employed under a contract of service. It has from time to time been urged that people who were self-employed should be brought within the scope of the Act and in a few marginal cases this has been done; but in general it has been felt that the conditions under which self-employed people work make it too difficult in case of an accident to decide whether it occurred in the course of their work or not and that the distinction between sickness benefit under the main scheme and injury benefit under the industrial injuries scheme would be impossible to maintain in their case. The small shopkeeper, for example, often lives over the shop and passes very quickly from his ordinary domestic affairs to the business of looking after the shop without any obvious change of environment that would serve to mark which he was engaged upon when, for example, he fell down and broke his leg.

The number of people insured under the Industrial Injuries Act (21 million of whom about one-third are women) is rather more than those insured in Class I under the main scheme. This is due to the fact that there are several differences in the scope of the two schemes; married women have to be insured for industrial injuries whether or not they choose to be insured for other benefits. On the other hand people insured under the main scheme in Class II or III are not included in the industrial injuries scheme nor are members of the armed forces, though the latter are included for many purposes under the main Act.

PAYMENT OF CONTRIBUTIONS

The broad rule is that everyone liable to pay contributions should pay a contribution each week unless he or she is drawing benefit for the whole of that week, but there are a number of special rules and exceptions too complicated to explain here. For weeks of sickness or unemployment the contributor will be given a credit, i.e. he will be regarded as having paid the contribution for that week.

Contributions are paid by or in respect of about 17 million people by means of national insurance stamps which can be bought at a Post Office and have to be stuck on to special cards provided by the Department. These cards have to be printed well in advance of the time when they will be used and as the rate of contribution is stated on the card a change in contribution rates can cause a certain amount of confusion; the desirability of omitting the rate from the cards has been considered but the balance of convenience seems to lie with the present arrangement which, for most of the time at any rate, tells the public what they have to pay.

Each card runs for 52 weeks and at the end of that period it has to be exchanged for a new one. To facilitate the handling of the 45 million or so cards involved in a complete exchange the insured population has been divided into four categories whose cards are of different colours and run from different dates. Cards in the first category run from March, in the second from June, in the third from September and in the fourth from December.

The preparation and exchange of cards is done by the local offices. When cards are due for exchange they have to prepare new cards for people living in their area, by writing the contributor's name and national insurance number on the cards. For employees of large firms new cards are written in advance. This work involves close co-operation with employers in the area and some of the work is done on their premises. To save men the trouble of calling at the local office, cards for the employees of a particular firm are usually exchanged by the firm in bulk.

The stamped card handed in in exchange for a new one is sent to Newcastle where the contributions it represents are posted to the contributor's individual record; as cards may have stamps worth anything up to £45 on them they are perforated to cancel the stamps and render them useless. The fraudulent removal of stamps for re-use has never assumed large proportions but there has been sufficient to make it necessary to have a special section whose sole task is to examine suspicious cards after they have been handed in to see whether any of the stamps have been tampered with.

Although affixing stamps to cards is the usual way of paying contributions, other methods are available which have the advantage for large employers that they do away with the necessity of holding large stocks of valuable stamps and having them stuck individually on cards. One such method involves the use of a specially designed machine which impresses a device on the card. The machine is fitted with a meter which can be set to permit a certain number of impressions to be made and the employer who wants to use this method 'buys' as many impressions as he requires. The machine is set accordingly by the local office and then sealed and the employer passes his cards through the machine week by week. Another method is based on the firm's payroll and the employer pays the amount due by cheque. About £200 million a year is collected by these two methods, representing the contributions due for about 5½ million employees, and their use is expected to increase as the many advantages become better known.

Although these alternative methods involve more accounting work for the Ministry there are compensatory advantages as they simplify the work of seeing that contributions are being duly paid.

The insured population has complied with its obligations in paying contributions in a remarkable way. This is perhaps just as well as it would, in practice, be impossible to take effective steps to see that 24 million contributions were being paid regularly every week. 'Compliance work', as the task of checking the payment of contributions is called in the Department, is now part of the work of the local offices and broadly speaking it is of two kinds. Inspectors regularly visit works and other business premises to inspect the cards held by the employer for his employees. The Inspectors used to work on a rotation system under which they visited every employer in their area every so often. Experience has shown that the routine and detailed inspection of the records of a large company wastes a lot of time as the payment of contributions is part of the routine of payment of wages and the company's auditors can be relied on to see that it is properly done. A rather more selective system was therefore adopted and this has been found to produce larger returns for the time spent on inspection.

The other kind of compliance work is the following up of cases where at the end of the contribution year the insured contributor has not handed in a card or has handed one in which is incompletely stamped. This work is highly organized and rather complicated. Each year about $3\frac{1}{2}$ million cards are handed in which, on a quick scrutiny, appear to be deficient and about another $\frac{3}{4}$ million contributors do not hand in a card at all. A blank space on a card or a missing card can, however, be explained in several ways in addition to simple failure to pay a contribution due; it may be that the contributor was sick or unemployed and failed to claim a 'credit' to which he was entitled; or if the contributor is a woman she may have married and ceased to be liable to pay. These are some of the possibilities and there are others too detailed to mention. Some cards have one or two contributions missing but tests have shown that while quite a lot of people occasionally default in this way very few make a habit of doing so. Many factors have to be taken into account in deciding how far it is worth pursuing defaulters. Where it is decided to do so a personal visit may be paid by an officer and if no satisfactory explanation is forthcoming the defaulter may be prosecuted or sued in the Courts for the amount due. A series of elaborate tests were made in order to find out to what extent the National Insurance Fund was losing money by reason of non-compliance by people who ought to pay and were in a position to do so. The upshot of these tests was that it was estimated that about £1¼ million a year more might be collected. This figure is about one-third of 1 per cent. of the amount collected in contributions and about half of it is due from people who missed one or two contributions; to put sustained pressure on them would cost a great deal more than the value of the missing contributions. The missing contributions are not in any case a total loss to the fund as an insured contributor who fails to pay his contributions may find, when he comes to claim benefit or pension, that he will get less than the normal rates and in extreme cases may be deprived of it entirely. In the presence of figures like these one is justified in saying that the public have accepted, and do value, the insurance method of providing themselves with financial aid in time of trouble.

F

CHAPTER VIII

Adjudication

*

GENERAL

THE schemes administered by the Ministry provide pensions and benefits that are legal rights to which anyone who fulfils the prescribed conditions is legally entitled. The machinery for deciding claims to pensions and benefits is therefore very important. It has never been the practice to commit the decision of claims to social benefits to the Courts of law; sometimes they have been decided by agencies like the Approved Societies under the National Health Insurance Scheme; sometimes they have been decided by the Minister like the original war pensions and sometimes by specially constituted tribunals. In the schemes administered by the Ministry a variety of methods is used.

Family allowances are decided by the Minister (or by the Department acting on his behalf) with an appeal to special legal referees and the possibility of a reference to the High Court on points of law. Claims to national insurance and industrial injury pensions and benefits are decided by specially appointed officers in the Department known as 'insurance officers' with an appeal to a local tribunal and a further appeal to a Commissioner, who is a lawyer of the highest standing appointed by the Crown; medical questions arising on claims under the Industrial Injuries Act are decided by medical boards with an appeal to a medical appeal tribunal. Questions relating to a person's insurability, his classification and the number of contributions he has paid are decided by the Minister with an appeal on points of law to the High Court. War pensions are decided by the Minister with an appeal to special tribunals appointed by the Lord Chancellor and provision for a reference to the High Court (in Scotland the Court of Session) on points of law.

This variety is largely a matter of history. The machinery for deciding war pensions had been built up over many years before the two Ministries were amalgamated, the ex-servicemen's representatives were satisfied with it and it would have been folly to change it. Family allowances were brought into operation before the National

Insurance Acts and before the machinery of local tribunals under those Acts had been set up; some method of settling disputes had to be provided and in the circumstances it was decided to adopt the centralized machinery then being used for contributory pensions. The system of insurance officer, local tribunal (formerly Court of Referees) and Commissioner (formerly Umpire), collectively known as 'the statutory authorities', was familiar and accepted in connection with unemployment benefit, and once it had been decided to abandon the idea of administering sickness benefit through the Approved Societies, who themselves decided claims with certain rights of appeal to the Minister, fresh machinery was needed and it was a natural step to use the same machinery as for unemployment benefit, with which sickness benefit would in future be more closely associated. It was also decided, partly on grounds of greater convenience to the claimant, to decentralize the appeal machinery for pensions and to bring it into line with the other benefits.

For a time questions of insurability under the unemployment insurance schemes, like claims to unemployment benefit, were decided by the Umpire, but it was found that this did not work very well, especially as many of these questions were common to national health insurance, in which, largely because of the absence of local office machinery, they were decided centrally with an appeal to a County Court. In 1920 the two procedures were brought into line and questions of insurability under both schemes were decided by the Minister with an appeal to the High Court on points of law. These arrangements were continued in the National Insurance Act and the National Insurance (Industrial Injuries) Act, 1946; partly because they had in fact been working well and had not given rise to complaint but also because the questions raised in these disputes are often of a general character more suited to final decision by the Courts of law than by the specialized system of tribunals adopted for benefit claims.

It is proposed in this chapter to deal with all these arrangements other than those for war pensions, which are described in the chapter dealing with that subject.

THE INSURANCE OFFICER

When a claim to benefit or pension is made under the National Insurance Act or the National Insurance (Industrial Injuries) Act it is referred to one of the specially appointed insurance officers for decision. There is at least one insurance officer in every local office and in the larger offices there may be several. Insurance officers are usually of executive officer or higher rank and are formally appointed for the purpose by the Minister. Although there is no appeal from one insurance officer to another there is a kind of hierarchy which, in conjunction with the publication of leading decisions by the National Insurance Commissioner, ensures a reasonable degree of uniformity in their work. At each regional headquarters there is a Regional Insurance Officer who ranks as an Assistant Regional Controller; his functions are to deal with difficult questions about which local insurance officers may feel in need of help and generally to supervise their work. At headquarters in London there is a Chief Insurance Officer; this is a special appointment usually held by a senior Assistant Secretary who draws extra pay while holding the post. He has a small staff who hold insurance officers' powers and, in addition to supervising the work of insurance officers throughout the Department, he is responsible for the preparation and presentation of cases which go before the National Insurance Commissioner on appeal from a local tribunal.

Although all these insurance officers are members of the staff of the Department there is a rigid rule that in deciding claims to benefit they act independently and that other officers, though superior in rank, cannot give them directions or overrule them. This rule, which is indeed the basis of the insurance officer system, is accepted by Ministers who have repeatedly stated in Parliament that they cannot interfere with decisions made by insurance officers.

Claims to unemployment benefit are still made at the Employment Exchanges and to deal with them members of the Exchange staffs are appointed to act as insurance officers. They work under the general supervision of Regional Insurance Officers in the regional headquarters of the Ministry of Labour and National Service who for this purpose are guided by the Chief Insurance Officer of the Ministry of Pensions and National Insurance who also deals with appeals to the National Insurance Commissioner on unemployment benefit questions.

Insurance officers do not hold oral hearings; they deal with claims on written material submitted by the claimant or collected by the appropriate Department. The claimant's employer or late employer is frequently asked for information about the circumstances of the claim; in industrial injury cases, for example, he will be asked for details of the alleged accident and in unemployment benefit cases why the man's employment came to an end. If the claim is allowed, and the vast majority of them are, the claimant will receive his benefit without any further formality; if it is disallowed he will be informed in writing, given reasons for the decision and told of his right to appeal to a local tribunal.

In certain circumstances the insurance officer may refer the claim to a tribunal without giving a decision. It was at one time a statutory rule that certain types of case where it looked as though a claimant to unemployment benefit might incur a penalty for leaving a job without good cause or for some other kind of industrial misconduct had to be referred in this way; there are no similar provisions in the existing scheme but it is always open to the insurance officer to refer a case if he thinks fit. Sometimes a claim will give rise to a special question which it is for the Minister to decide, or in an industrial injury case to a medical question. In such cases the insurance officer must refer that question to the appropriate authority and only when he has received its decision can he proceed to give a decision on the claim as a whole.

The most common special questions are those relating to whether a child can be claimed as a dependant, to the payment of contributions and, in claims to disablement pensions, to the degree of disablement. Questions relating to dependent children are dealt with under the family allowance machinery and the way in which the other questions are decided is described below.

THE LOCAL TRIBUNAL

Every claimant whose claim is disallowed by an insurance officer is entitled to appeal to a local tribunal and no leave to appeal is required. There are nearly 220 local tribunals each of which exercises jurisdiction in an area comprising several local office areas. For convenience the local tribunal is centred on one of the larger offices in the area and the arrangements for convening a tribunal, for securing the attendance of witnesses and for attending the sitting are made from that office.

Local tribunals consist of three persons. The chairman is practically always a lawyer who has been appointed by the Minister after consultation with the Lord Chancellor in England and Wales and with the Lord Advocate in Scotland (the only exceptions have been some very experienced chairmen of the former Courts of Referees); he is paid a fee for each session. The other members are chosen, as far as possible in rotation, from two panels of persons constituted by the Minister after consultation with the Local Advisory Committee for the locality; one panel consists of persons representing employers, and for national insurance cases includes self-employed persons; the other panel represents employed persons. In making up the panels employers' associations, trade unions, local authorities, friendly societies and similar bodies are consulted.

Chairmen are appointed for three years but usually continue in office until they reach the age of 72 when they are expected to retire. To preserve the impartiality of the tribunals it is laid down that a chairman's appointment may be terminated if he becomes a paid official of an association of employers or employed persons or takes a prominent part in national politics, or if he or the firm to which he belongs engages to a substantial extent in legal work connected with national insurance matters or with actions between work-people and their employers.

Members of panels also hold office for three years at a time and their appointment, too, may be terminated if they undertake work inconsistent with their status as a member of a tribunal; if, for example, a panel member becomes a candidate for Parliament his appointment will be terminated, indeed if it were not, he might incur penalties as although members of a tribunal other than the chairman are not paid fees, they receive expenses and compensation for loss of wages.

Most tribunals sit once a week and they may sit more frequently if the work requires. When a tribunal is required, the clerk, who is an officer of the Department, notifies the member of each panel next on the rota and the tribunal is constituted when the chairman and the other two members assemble; with the consent of the claimant a tribunal may consist of the chairman only or the chairman and one other member.

Claimants who have appealed against the insurance officer's decision on their claims are notified in writing of the time and place when their appeal will be heard. Neither the Press nor the general public are allowed to attend hearings of national insurance appeals; this is a practice of long standing based on the view that such cases often involve domestic and other personal details which it might be embarrassing for a claimant to discuss in public. Industrial injury appeals, on the other hand, are heard in public, largely because of the tradition of hearing workmen's compensation cases in open court.

General rules of procedure for tribunals are laid down in regulations but a good deal of discretion is left to the chairman in conducting the proceedings. The procedure is usually fairly informal but it varies to some extent from one tribunal to another as some chairmen are inclined to be more formal than others. The tribunal is furnished with the written documents in the case, the claimant's grounds for appealing, the insurance officer's statement of his reasons for the original decision and any other information he may have had before him in reaching it. There may be oral argument and further evidence may be produced; witnesses are not sworn. If in any case before a tribunal a 'special' question arises, that is to say a question which falls to be decided by the Minister or a medical question, they must refer that question to the appropriate authority and adjourn the hearing until the decision on it is received.

A claimant may be accompanied by a friend who may put his case to the tribunal for him; in national insurance cases legal representation is not allowed but in industrial injury cases a claimant may, with the chairman's consent, be represented by a lawyer. In practice very few claimants to industrial injury benefits take advantage of this rule, which owes its origin to workmen's compensation practice.

A tribunal usually announces its decision at the end of the hearing and then records it in writing giving reasons. If the tribunal is not unanimous the decision of the majority prevails, but the dissenting member must give his reasons for dissent; with a tribunal of two the chairman has a second or casting vote. No costs are awarded, even where a claimant in an industrial injury case is legally represented, but claimants and their witnesses are paid travelling expenses and subsistence allowances and also an allowance if they have lost wages as the result of attending the hearing.

Nearly half the cases which have come before the appeal tribunals have related to claims to unemployment benefit. In 1956, for example, tribunals heard some 43,000 cases of which just on 19,000 were unemployment benefit claims. The next most common type of case is the claim to sickness benefit, of which there were nearly 12,500 in 1956; retirement pensions only gave rise to 1,700 appeals most of which probably related to the retirement condition. In the same year there were 7,000 appeals in industrial injury cases. Formidable as these figures may sound, it must be remembered that well over 11 million claims to these benefits and pensions were received in the year.

THE COMMISSIONER

The final court of appeal established by the National Insurance Acts is the National Insurance Commissioner. The National Insurance (Industrial Injuries) Act also set up a National Insurance (Industrial Injuries) Commissioner, but in practice the two offices are combined. There is one Commissioner for the whole of Great Britain who sits in London and five Deputy Commissioners of whom one works in Edinburgh, one in Cardiff and the other three in London. The Commissioner and Deputy Commissioners are appointed by Royal Warrant under the Sign Manual and must be Barristers or Advocates of at least ten years' standing; they hold office during good behaviour. The posts are usually full-time but one Deputy may be appointed on a part-time basis. The Commissioner and the full-time Deputies are pensionable on substantially the same conditions as County Court Judges. The Commissioner and the Deputy Commissioners are appointed on the recommendation of the Lord Chancellor.

Persons whose claims to benefit or pension have been rejected by a local tribunal can make a further appeal to the Commissioner but in many cases leave must first be obtained either from the tribunal or from the Commissioner. The national insurance rules about leave to appeal were based on the old rules that governed the right of appeal from the Court of Referees to the Umpire in unemployment benefit cases. If the tribunal is unanimous in rejecting the claim the claimant can only appeal with leave, but an association to which he belongs or the insurance officer may appeal without leave. If the tribunal was not unanimous the claimant, too, can appeal without having to obtain leave. An application for leave to appeal must first be made to the tribunal, but if they refuse the Commissioner may be asked to grant it. The industrial injury rules are different. Leave is required in every case, whether the decision was unanimous or not, and not only by the claimant but also by the insurance officer and an association.

The Commissioner holds an oral hearing whenever he thinks it necessary or the claimant with reasonable grounds asks for it. At these hearings the claimant and the insurance officer are entitled, under both schemes, to be represented by a lawyer. Hearings of industrial injury appeals are open to the public; in other cases the admission of the public is at the discretion of the Commissioner. The case on behalf of the Department is usually presented by one of the Chief Insurance Officer's staff but on occasion, if the claimant is represented by Counsel, the Chief Insurance Officer will be represented by a member of the legal branch of the Department; legal representation is more common in industrial injury cases than in other types of claim. Where both parties are legally represented the proceedings before the Commissioner may be conducted with much the same degree of formality as an arbitration before a legal arbitrator; if the claimant conducts his own case the proceedings may be quite informal.

The Commissioner gives his decision in writing and almost always gives a reasoned judgment. In specially difficult cases under either Act the Commissioner may sit as a tribunal with two Deputy Commissioners and in the event of disagreement the decision of the majority prevails. Copies of the Commissioner's decisions are sent to the claimant and the Commissioner also selects certain decisions, which in his view establish points of importance, and these are published by the Stationery Office for the guidance of the statutory authorities and the information of the public. No costs are awarded either to or against claimants but allowances on the same scale as for appearances before tribunals are paid to claimants and witnesses.

Although the decisions of the Commissioner are declared by the Act to be 'final' it is now clear that the High Court will, under its general supervisory powers over lesser courts and tribunals, set one of his decisions aside if, on an application being made to it, it comes to the conclusion that it contains an error of law. An application of this kind was made to the Divisional Court but as the Court agreed with the Commissioner's decision the question whether they would have set it aside if they had come to the opposite view was expressly reserved. Since then, the question has come before the Court of Appeal on an application to set aside the decisions of a Medical Appeal Tribunal under the Industrial Injuries Act whose decisions are also declared to be final, and the Court held that if there was an error of law on the face of the decision they had jurisdiction to set it aside notwithstanding the Act declared the decision to be final.

The system of 'statutory authorities' (the insurance officer, the local tribunal and the Commissioner) was derived from that set up by the Unemployment Insurance Acts. It is certainly expeditious in comparison, for example, with the time taken to get a final decision from the House of Lords in a workmen's compensation case and it is undeniably less expensive to the applicant. An idea of the use which claimants make of their right of appealing to the Commissioner can be gleaned from the figures for 1956. In that year there were about 1,600 appeals, of which 600 were decided in the claimant's favour. About 520 of these appeals were unemployment benefit cases, 260 related to sickness benefit and 660 were industrial injury cases. The much higher proportion of industrial injury appeals in comparison with the total number of such cases reflects the greater legal complexity of the industrial injuries scheme.

MINISTER'S QUESTIONS

Of the questions reserved for the Minister's decision under the National Insurance Act, the most important are those relating to the class in which a person is insurable and whether he or his employer has paid the contributions due. These questions are only referred for formal decision when some doubt has been raised about them. Doubts may arise either on a claim to benefit or in connection with proceedings in Court for non-payment of contributions, or when an insured person or his employer wants to be certain about his position in relation to insurance under the Act. Any question whether a person is insurable under the Industrial Injuries Act is dealt with in the same way.

Other questions that involve an element of discretion, for example whether a constant attendance allowance is payable under the industrial injuries scheme, are also Minister's questions but these seldom give rise to formal proceedings.

Questions for the Minister generally originate in a local office on a claim to benefit or as the result of oral or written enquiry by someone who wants to know how he stands under the insurance scheme. If the facts are in dispute or doubtful a local enquiry is ordered and this happens in about three-quarters of the cases decided. The enquiry is usually held by a member of the Department's legal staff and the procedure at the hearing is fairly formal; legal representation is allowed and evidence may be given on oath. The person holding the enquiry makes a report to the Department which forms the basis of the formal decision; the report is not published. The Minister's decision is made in writing and reasons are given on request; many of them are on special facts of interest only to a particular individual but others raise general issues such as whether certain working arrangements amount to a contract of service, in which case the man is insurable in Class I, or to a contract for services, when he would be in Class II. A selection of the more important decisions are published by the Stationery Office, continuing a series started under the earlier Acts.

A person who is dissatisfied with the Minister's decision in his case can appeal on a point of law to a single judge of the High Court in England or to the Court of Session in Scotland; the decision of this judge is final. Proceedings on an appeal, which in England is by way of 'case stated' and by the corresponding procedure in Scotland are governed by Rules of Court. The judge has power to award costs and may order the Minister to pay them even though his decision is upheld; this enables points of general interest to be fully argued without involving the person concerned in expense. The Minister rarely asks for costs. In the last five years there have been seven appeals to the Courts, in all of which the decision given by the Minister was upheld; in the same period over 8,000 formal decisions were given by the Department.

Questions about the number of contributions an insured contributor has paid are usually answered by reference to the records at Newcastle, but if there is a dispute about payment an enquiry may be held to enable the contributor to produce evidence showing that he did in fact pay the contributions said to be missing; such cases are rare.

MEDICAL BOARDS

For the purpose of a claim to disablement benefit under the Industrial Injuries Act questions relating to whether an accident has resulted in any disability and to the degree of disablement for the purpose of a claim to disablement benefit are reserved for the decision of medical boards with an appeal to a medical appeal tribunal. Medical boards also serve as the final authority on the diagnosis of an industrial disease.

There are about 120 medical boarding centres distributed through the country, of which 29 are special centres dealing with pneumoconiosis. A medical board consists as a general rule of two doctors, though for certain limited purposes a single doctor may, with the claimant's consent, act as a board; if a board of two doctors disagrees the claimant may be re-examined by a board of three doctors and in the event of further disagreement the opinion of the majority prevails.

The procedure at a medical board is essentially that of a clinical examination of the claimant. As a rule, therefore, only the claimant is present, unless exceptionally the board think it advisable that he or she should be accompanied by a friend or relative. The board have before them all that is known of the man's medical history, including any reports by specialists, X-ray films and so on which may have been obtained for the purpose of the claim and may help the board to reach their conclusions on the man's condition.

The board record in writing their decision and a statement of their findings of fact; a copy of the decision and a summary of the findings are sent to the claimant. There is no provision for awarding costs but the usual expenses and allowances are paid.

An assessment of disablement made by a medical board may either be 'final' if the doctors think the claimant's condition has stabilized sufficiently to justify a final view of the extent of the injury likely to result from his accident, or it may be provisional for any period the board may specify. Where a provisional award is given the claimant is automatically re-boarded before the end of the period specified in the award to see whether any further awards should be made. There was a tendency at first to make provisional awards for unduly short periods. With more experience boards are giving provisional awards for longer periods, thus saving the claimant from the inconvenience and possible strain of frequent medical examinations.

Where the board make a final award the claimant is entitled to appeal to a medical appeal tribunal. There is no right of appeal against a provisional award before the end of two years from the first reference to the board nor when the duration of the award falls wholly within that period. There are, however, special provisions under which any decision of a medical board (including those from which there is no appeal) may at the Minister's discretion be referred to a medical appeal tribunal at any time and this provision has been freely used to enable cases to be considered by the appeal tribunals where the claimant had no right of appeal but it was obvious that the case ought to be further considered.

MEDICAL APPEAL TRIBUNALS

There are fourteen medical appeal tribunals, each of which is presided over by a barrister or advocate of high standing appointed after consultation with the Lord Chancellor or in Scotland with the Lord Advocate, and has two other members who are eminent physicians or surgeons selected for the London tribunal after consultation with the heads of the Royal Colleges of Physicians and Surgeons and for the other tribunals with the heads of the University Medical Schools. The Department provides a clerk who makes all the necessary arrangements for convening the tribunal and for the attendance of claimants. The procedure of the medical appeal tribunals is rather more formal than that of the medical boards, but it varies considerably from one tribunal to another, some chairmen being given to a greater degree of formality than others. Medical appeal tribunals usually work on the basis of the medical documents in the case. They may call for specialists' reports and the medical members may examine the claimant for themselves; it is exceptional for oral evidence other than that of the claimant himself to be given. Legal arguments may be heard on such questions as the application of the regulations governing the assessment of disability for the purpose of the Act and the claimant may be legally represented; only in very exceptional cases is the Minister represented by a lawyer but an officer of the Department attends to place the issues before the tribunal.

The tribunal record their decision in writing and include a statement of their reasons and the findings of fact on which their decision is based. The decision of a medical appeal tribunal is declared by the Act to be final, but it is now clear that it is subject to review by the Courts for error of law.

The arrangements for convening medical boards and medical appeal tribunals under the industrial injuries scheme and the preparation of cases for them are carried out from regional headquarters by lay staff working in close co-operation with the regional medical staff. The volume of the work is steadily increasing and as it is rare for a medical board to give a final award in the first instance there is a growing number of cases which have to be periodically reviewed; it will be many years before the number of cases dealt with annually by the boards and tribunals is stabilized. In 1951 under 200,000 cases were dealt with by medical boards and by 1956 the number had risen to over 300,000. The number of appeals to the medical appeal tribunals has also increased; in 1951 there were just over 9,000 and in 1956 there were 14,500.

FAMILY ALLOWANCES REFEREES

Claims to family allowances are decided by the Department ('the Minister') in the first instance and the vast majority of claims are admitted without question. Out of over $2\frac{1}{4}$ million claims received when the scheme was launched about 2 or 3 per cent. were rejected and many of these related to families with only one child about which there could really be no argument; by 1951 the number rejected had dropped below 1 per cent.

Appeals against the Minister's decision in family allowance cases are decided by barristers or advocates appointed as referees by the Minister after consultation with the Lord Chancellor's Department. There are ten referees, one of whom, the senior referee, receives an annual payment; the others receive fees and the Scottish referees also receive an annual retainer. The number of appeals during 1956 was about 1,700 of which rather less than half were successful.

One of the legal officers of the Department acts as Registrar, and the senior referee exercises a rather loose control: he may, for example, arrange to sit with two of his colleagues to decide questions of special difficulty. Most of the appeals are decided on the written documents, which include a statement by the claimant of the grounds of appeal and, usually, an answer by the Minister. In about 10 per cent. of the appeals the referee holds a local oral hearing. This is held in private but the claimant is entitled to bring someone to help her in presenting her case and she may be legally represented. The proceedings are kept informal though witnesses may be sworn if the referee so decides. The referee puts his decision in writing and he almost invariably sets out the material facts and his reasons.

There is no appeal from the decision of a referee, but provision is made for obtaining a ruling on a point of law from the High Court or in Scotland the Court of Session. Since the Act came into force two cases have been referred in this way and in both of them the original decision was confirmed by the Court.

CHAPTER IX

Administration

*

WHEN the new social security plans were being worked out by the Coalition Government in 1944 a great deal of thought was given to the best method of administering them. Of the existing schemes some were administered directly by the Central Government; the contributory pensions scheme, for example, was administered by the Ministry of Health and unemployment insurance by the Ministry of Labour and National Service. National health insurance, the forerunner of sickness benefit and the National Health Service, was administered by non-governmental agencies known as Approved Societies. The idea behind the Approved Society type of administration was to make use of the existing friendly societies who were already paying sickness benefit, but provision was also made for industrial insurance companies and trade unions to participate and the latter eventually played a very important part in the administration of the scheme. Workmen's compensation, to be replaced by the new industrial injury benefit, was under the general supervision of the Home Office, which was formerly responsible for the Factory Inspectorate and other measures aimed at reducing the number of industrial accidents. Claims for workmen's compensation were usually handled by insurance companies or, in some industries, mutual insurance societies formed for the purpose and disputes were settled in the Courts.

To have left the administration of the new schemes divided up between so many different agencies would have been out of keeping with the grand conception of a unified and co-ordinated plan. Careful consideration was given to the possibility of employing the Approved Societies either in their existing or some modified form as paying agents for at least some of the benefits, and the arguments for and against this course are set out in the Coalition Government's White Paper on Social Insurance (Part I) (Cmd. 6550). In the end it was decided to consolidate the administration of the whole scheme, including the new family allowances, under one organization. There was still the possibility of using for this purpose a non-ministerial administrative board on the lines of the Assistance Board, which, after a somewhat difficult start, had re-established itself in the confidence of the public, largely as the result of its administration of supplementary pensions for old age pensioners and of war-time schemes such as that usually known by its initials as P.R.D. (the Prevention and Relief of Distress) and the scheme for providing immediate payments to air raid victims. The Coalition Government came to the conclusion that the launching of the new schemes would involve so much Parliamentary activity that it was essential to entrust it in the early stages to a Ministry, but their White Paper expressly reserved the possibility that the administration might be transferred to a Board when the schemes were in operation and administrative policy clearly defined and established. The Labour Government agreed that ministerial administration was essential when they came to draft their legislation in 1946 and so far at least no serious consideration has ever been given to the possibility of transferring the administration to a Board.

Once it was decided to entrust the administration to a Ministry, it was fairly obvious that none of the existing Departments would be able to administer a general scheme that included such diverse elements as unemployment benefit, sickness benefit, industrial injury benefits and family allowances. The Ministry of Health could not handle unemployment benefit, the Ministry of Labour and National Service was too much concerned with manpower problems to take on sickness benefit or family allowances and the intention to have common rates for pensions and benefits made it difficult to parcel out responsibility among several Departments.

It was therefore decided that a new Ministry should be set up for the purpose and the first step towards bringing the new social security plans into being was the establishment in 1944 of the Ministry of National Insurance. There remained the choice between a centralized administration operating through some huge central office that would conduct all its business through the post and a system of local offices. The Ministry of Labour with its Employment Exchanges and the Assistance Board and the Ministry of Food with their local offices had proved the value, in the administration of social services affecting large numbers of people, of local points of contact to which the public could come and have their problems examined and dealt with on the spot. There are serious risks in trying to handle, through a central machine, large numbers of claims by the public which must be dealt with promptly. The sheer weight of paper which such an organization accumulates creates its own difficulties and if things do go wrong the ensuing delay brings still more correspondence from dissatisfied claimants, which adds to the confusion and can quickly produce chaos. Local offices avoid these troubles. The amount of business transacted by even a hard-pressed local office is of manageable proportions. Extra casual staff can be recruited locally; help can be given by other offices with less work on hand and should a local office be in danger of breaking down, arrangements can be made to transfer part of its work elsewhere.

The decision to administer the new schemes through local offices was undoubtedly right but the decision to set up a new chain of local offices instead of using existing offices belonging to other Departments has often been criticized.

From the outset one exception to the plan of administering the new schemes through local offices belonging to the new Ministry was accepted. Although the new Ministry would be responsible for policy questions connected with unemployment benefit, the day-to-day administration of that service was to continue to be carried on by the Employment Exchanges of the Ministry of Labour and National Service as agents for the new Ministry. The main reason for this was the close connection between the 'placing' (or job finding) work of that Department and the act of claiming unemployment benefit.

Two policy decisions introduced further complications in planning the new organization. It was decided to start the new family allowances scheme and to introduce the new retirement pensions in advance of the other benefits and before the local office organization could be set up. It was also contemplated at one time that the new industrial injuries scheme might be brought into operation in advance of the main scheme and tentative plans were made for administering it through two hundred offices to be specially set up for the purpose. This idea was abandoned largely because it was doubtful whether all the arrangements required for the new scheme, and especially the machinery of medical boards and medical appeal tribunals, could be got ready sufficiently far in advance of the main scheme to make it worth while facing all the complications that would have arisen if one of two closely related schemes had been brought into operation before the other. In the end the National Insurance Act and the National Insurance (Industrial Injuries) Act were brought into operation on the same date.

When the new Ministry of National Insurance was set up in November, 1944, it faced a formidable programme. It had to prepare and pilot through Parliament the legislation creating the new system of social security. It had to fashion the completely new family allowances scheme and create machinery to run it; it had to prepare and lay before Parliament a long and complicated series of regulations which would be required to fill in the gaps in the National Insurance Acts, and especially in the main National Insurance Act which was deliberately streamlined to facilitate its passage through Parliament; arrangements had to be made for taking over beneficiaries under the old schemes together with their records and for winding up some 1,000 Approved Societies with over 6,000 branches and, above all, it had to set up a large number of local offices with the necessary backing of records and other central organizations. The staff, which at its peak numbered over 39,000, had to be recruited, posted and trained.

It was essential, if the new schemes were to get off to a good start, that the 25 million or so people who would be affected by them as contributors or potential beneficiaries should know in good time what their responsibilities and rights were. Shortly before the Appointed Day, therefore, the Ministry undertook an extensive publicity campaign. Its main feature was the distribution to over 14 million households between the 24th May and 12th June, 1948, of a 32-page booklet or *Family Guide to National Insurance*. This took some time to print and distribute, so it had to be prepared long before many of the detailed provisions of the various schemes had been settled. It could therefore only deal in simple terms with the main points and, even so, some risks were taken in making it available so early. An edition was published in Welsh and a Polish translation was also made available at local offices and employment exchanges. *The Family Guide* was gradually supplemented by leaflets containing more detailed information and by July, 1949, some 50 million leaflets had been published. Further publicity was provided through lectures given by lecturers supplied by the Central Office of Information at meetings arranged by organizations like the Women's Institutes and Rotary Clubs and over 1,500 meetings of workers at factories all over the country were addressed by members of the Ministry's staff. A special film was exhibited at over 3,000 cinemas and the Press and the B.B.C. co-operated generously and, as the Appointed Day approached, devoted much space and time to explaining the details of the new schemes. It was largely due to the great care taken over this advance publicity that, when the Appointed Day eventually arrived, the new arrangements came into operation with a minimum of trouble.

For a time, special campaigns were continued explaining such things as the necessity of always quoting an insurance number when claiming benefit and when and how to exchange contribution cards. As the public became familiar with the new arrangements the need for this special publicity gradually ceased.

It proved no easy task to find a thousand premises for local offices in a country which was just emerging from a destructive war and resort was had to improvisation by adapting chapels, warehouses, huts and similar buildings which had not been designed as offices.

G

In order to provide the local offices with the staff they needed many people had to move from one place to another and often found themselves in difficulties over new accommodation. Sometimes these moves caused real personal hardship, but these difficulties were gradually overcome and the staff settled down. The frequency with which questions connected with housing and accommodation for the staff appeared on the agenda of Whitley discussions in the early days is, in itself, an interesting commentary on the problems which confronted the new Ministry. The Newcastle office, with a staff that at one time reached nearly 9,000, also gave rise to serious accommodation problems. A completely new block of offices extending over 64 acres had to be built for the staff to work in. The serious shortage of houses at Newcastle, which had suffered severely from air raids, made it impossible to obtain homes for the staff in anything like the numbers needed. To accommodate them temporarily hostels were set up and at one time as many as 800 were accommodated in this way. But here too, thanks to the goodwill of the local housing authorities who provided 700 houses for the staff brought in from other parts, the position steadily improved and at the end of 1956 only 80 members of the staff were still living in hostels; though many others have had to go long distances to find homes of their own.

It is against the background of these years of effort and improvisation that the existing organization of the Ministry must be judged. When the National Insurance Bills were going through Parliament, many speakers emphasized the importance of making sure that the new schemes would be administered in the proper spirit and from the outset the new ministry was very much in the public eye. Plenty of people were suspicious of civil service administration and doubtful of the ability of civil servants to handle humanely the large section of the public that would resort to the Ministry in sickness, injury and old age, and they would not hesitate to ventilate any shortcomings that might be brought to their notice. These fears have been confounded by experience; considering the enormous number of claims that have been made on the Ministry, it is remarkable how few and far between have been complaints about the treatment that members of the public have received at the Ministry's hands. It is perhaps permissible to recall that, on more than one occasion, handsome tributes have been paid in Parliament to the way in which the Ministry carries on its business.

THE TRANSITIONAL PHASE

As the existing schemes of contributory pensions and national health insurance were to be wound up, the new Ministry was faced at the outset with a complicated transitional problem involving the transfer of nearly 4 million old age pensioners drawing the old 10s. pension to the new retirement pension and the taking over from the Approved Societies administering the National Health Insurance scheme of over three quarters of a million people drawing sickness benefit. For a time the Ministry had to administer not only the sickness benefit of the Approved Societies but also a wide variety of additional benefits such as dental and ophthalmic benefit which were in due course handed over to the National Health Service. As from the Appointed Day all current claims for sickness and disablement benefit would have to be reassessed at the new rates. The Approved Societies themselves had to be wound up and their records and many of their staff taken over. All this would have to be done without interrupting the regular payment of benefits and pensions.

Although the new schemes as a whole did not start until 1948 the Government announced during the second reading of the National Insurance Bill that the new retirement pensions would be introduced by the winter of 1946. This involved not merely a change in the rate of pension but also an enquiry to find out whether the pensioner had retired from regular work and so satisfied the new retirement condition. These enquiries had to be made locally to be effective and as the new Ministry had not yet been able to set up its own local offices the work was done on an agency basis by the Assistance Board and the Ministry of Labour and National Service. The introduction of the new pensions fell into two parts. Every week about 8,000 people qualified for the new pension and these were dealt with directly under the new scheme as they made their claims. There were also some $1\frac{1}{2}$ million existing pensioners between the ages to which the retirement condition applied and about $2\frac{1}{2}$ million pensioners over the ages of 70 for men and 65 for women who, though not liable to the retirement condition, would have to have their pension books up-rated as from the Appointed Day. This is the kind of task that the Ministry has learned by experience to take in its stride, but it was a very different matter to carry it through without a local office organization. At the time the pension administration was concentrated at Blackpool, Edinburgh and Cardiff and the sheer weight of numbers made itself felt. There were many anxious moments for the new Ministry but in the end the great majority of the pensioners received their new books well in advance of the day when the new pensions started to be payable.

The transfer of sickness benefit administration from the Approved Societies to the new Ministry was an even bigger and more complicated task. There were three main types of Approved Societies: the industrial assurance societies which, though few in number, covered the majority of the insured population and usually employed agents who often combined private insurance business with State business in periodical visits to members' homes; the trade union societies based on the trade unions to which they were attached and the friendly societies, which formed the largest group of separate administrative units and varied in size between societies with over three-quarters of a million members to those with a hundred or less. Friendly societies employed several widely differing methods of administration. Some worked through agents on much the same lines as the industrial assurance societies; some had no personal contact with their members and did all their business through the post; others, and these were perhaps most typical of the true spirit of the friendly society, held weekly meetings of members at the 'Lodge', 'Court' or 'Branch' at which the business was done.

In addition to members of Approved Societies there were what were known as 'fund members' under the old scheme. These were people who did not, or sometimes owing to a bad health record could not, join a society. They became 'deposit contributors' with limited rights to benefit depending on the amount they had paid in in contributions. Their rights were administered directly by the Health Departments from Blackpool, Edinburgh and Cardiff.

In all, over 6,000 separate administrative units had to be dealt with, and their records, which included the contribution records for the contributory pension scheme had to be taken over with many of their staff. A start was made with the arrangements for transferring the records in August, 1946. Long before the details of the new scheme could be foreseen with any certainty new record sheets were designed for transcribing the existing records to a form in which they could be used as the basis of the new scheme. Shortly afterwards the administration of the deposit contributors referred to above was decentralized to 43 newly established local offices. This involved the working out of procedures for operating a new type local office in conjunction with a central record branch which was to set the pattern for the future. These 43 local offices formed the nucleus around which the whole local office structure was eventually built. In due course they took over their quota of Approved Societies and sent out trained staff who helped to set up new offices, which in turn took over more societies and so the network of local offices gradually spread throughout the country.

The work of taking over from the Approved Societies started in earnest in the autumn of 1947 and was divided into two stages. First societies with less than 50,000 members were dealt with; this group included all except about 45 of the societies affected. In their case the take-over involved, in effect, the appointment of the Ministry as managers of their affairs, though they continued to exist as legal entities until the day appointed for the start of the new scheme. During this stage the Ministry's offices were involved in all the complications of the various schemes of additional benefits that the societies had provided. The work was allocated to the local offices as they were set up and it was frequently necessary to re-allocate it as fresh offices came into existence. This stage was effectively completed by the end of March, 1948, when work began on the remaining 45 societies who between them accounted for about 13 million members. In their case the arrangements were rather different. They were not transferred in the same way as the smaller societies had been. Their central offices continued to receive and award claims and they also continued to administer their schemes of additional benefits, but the payment of benefits awarded was taken over by the new local offices. Their records were in due course transferred direct to the Ministry's new central Record Office at Newcastle.

By the time the Appointed Day (5th July, 1948) arrived the local office organization was ready and the concluding stages of the take-over were completed without undue difficulty. The whole operation called for careful timing and close attention to detail, but it was completed successfully with a minimum amount of inconvenience to the beneficiaries, the people most concerned.

The winding up of the societies also involved complicated negotiations over premises and other assets, but these were carried through with the utmost good-will on the part of the societies which, however much they may have opposed the decision to exclude them from the administration of the new scheme, loyally accepted the decision once Parliament had given it and co-operated to the full in the task of making it effective.

GENERAL PLAN

A diagram showing the general administrative plan is given in Appendix V. The basic idea is that the Ministry's business with the public is done at the local offices of which there are now about 900 including 26 war pension offices taken over from the Ministry of Pensions. It is to the local office that the member of the public goes or writes if he wants advice about benefits and contributions or if he wants to claim any of the benefits, pensions or allowances, other than unemployment benefit which must be claimed at the Employment Exchange.

The nature of the schemes administered by the Department is such that they must be applied uniformly and there is very little scope for local discretion; conditions for benefit must be interpreted in the same way everywhere and the pensioner at Wick must get his pension on the same terms as the pensioner at Penzance. Nor is there much room for local variations in the management of a staff organized on civil service lines. Staff rules and conditions of service must be applied uniformly and the kind of work expected from each grade of staff must be the same everywhere; for example, the principal unit of command is the local office and the same grade of officer will be in charge of a local office of similar size and importance in every part of the country.

Means for co-ordinating the work and management of local offices had therefore to be provided. On the benefit side this is done through the adjudication machinery described in Chapter VIII, which ensures uniformity in the administration of pensions and benefits throughout the country. On the management side co-ordination depends on the Controllers in Scotland and Wales and the Regional Controllers in England, who, under the general directions of Headquarters, are responsible for the efficiency of the local office organization in their regions.

The Minister and Parliamentary Secretaries, as well as the Permanent Secretary and the senior members of the administrative staff, are located in London, but following the general policy of removing as much government business as possible from London, much of the work that is essentially headquarters or central in character is carried out at offices at Newcastle and Blackpool. Thus most of the war pensions work is done at Blackpool; family allowances work, the maintenance of the national insurance records and the preparation and issue of pension order books are all done at Newcastle.

With a three-tier organization of this kind the chain of command is all-important. When headquarters decides to send out instructions affecting local offices they are sent direct to the local offices and not through the regional headquarters; this ensures that all local offices get identical instructions on matters of general importance. Regional headquarters get copies of headquarters instructions and they also send out instructions of their own on local matters. When the local offices were first set up local experiments in methods of arranging work were encouraged as being the quickest way of finding out the best and most economical method of running them. But as the Ministry acquired experience, local experiments gave way to instructions from headquarters which, while permitting variations dictated by local conditions such as any peculiarity in the premises in which an office is housed, laid down the general lines for the arrangement of work in a local office.

If a local office is in any difficulty over an individual case it will usually consult its regional office who, in turn, will consult headquarters if necessary. But in urgent cases, or where a question has been raised with headquarters, by a Member of Parliament for example, a local office and headquarters will communicate direct with each other. This direct communication is sometimes inevitable, especially when questions have been asked in Parliament to which an immediate reply must be given, but unless the regional office is kept informed of what is happening in matters of importance it can lead to confusion.

Considerable use is made of the conference method in bringing about the necessary degree of uniformity in administration. Meetings of local office managers are regularly held by the Controllers at which difficulties are discussed and experience pooled. These meetings are sometimes attended by senior officers who want to hear the views of managers on some question under consideration at headquarters. Regular conferences are also held at headquarters. Medical officers, insurance officers, finance officers and other specialist officers from the regional headquarters all hold regular meetings under the chairmanship of a senior officer at headquarters to discuss their special subjects. In addition there are regular conferences of Regional Controllers, at which the chair is usually taken by the Deputy Secretary. At these meetings Controllers are told of matters which, although not calling for action at the moment, may involve local offices later on. Alternative courses and the ever-important question of the timing of some impending operation may be discussed with the object of discovering the plan likely to be most convenient to local offices within the limits imposed by considerations of general policy. The Controllers for their part raise questions which are causing trouble in the Regions and the ensuing discussion enables the experiences of other Controllers to be tapped and made available. Special sessions are held under the chairmanship of the Director of Establishments and Organization for the discussion of staff matters. Executive decisions are seldom given at these meetings. Where local office action is involved, decisions are conveyed by headquarters instructions issued in the ordinary way and instructions are also sent to Controllers embodying any conclusions reached at the conference that call for action on their part. These conferences afford useful opportunities for the discussion of matters which cannot very well be dealt with by correspondence and they are especially valuable when large-scale operations are being planned.

THE LOCAL OFFICE

At the end of 1956 the Ministry had 874 local national insurance offices. At one time there were nearly 1,000, but the number has gradually been reduced by closing smaller offices that seemed to be redundant. Local offices are so sited as to ensure that as far as possible every member of the public has an office within reasonable distance.

Local offices vary in size from the small rural office with a staff of 5 or 6 to the large office in a busy town which may have a staff of 100 or more. There has been a good deal of discussion about the most economical size for a local office and opinions have differed sharply. In general it will be found that the paper work of a very small office could be done more economically by combining offices into larger units; but paper work is by no means everything and even if the number of visitors is small it means a great deal to a rural community to have an office within reasonable distance. In some rural areas a compromise has been found by concentrating the paper work and opening full- or part-time 'caller offices' to which the public can come for advice on insurance matters. Very large offices are not as economical as one might expect, owing to difficulties of management and the number of senior staff needed for supervision. It is now generally accepted that the best and most economical unit all round is the office with a staff of about 35.

Many methods of organizing the work in local offices have been tried. They have varied between what might be called the 'moving belt' system where no one, except a few people employed on the counter to deal with callers and similar work or in the registry, works on more than one type of benefit and each person carries out one of successive stages in dealing with one type of claim, and the 'group system' where small teams of 8 or 10 deal with several benefits having features in common, for example, sickness, industrial injury and maternity benefit claims. The essential processes in dealing with a claim to benefit are opening a 'benefit unit' which is, in effect, a personal file for the particular claimant, though this is not always necessary as in the course of time a local office accumulates units for a large number of its regular customers; ascertaining from the Newcastle Records Branch the claimant's contribution record by sending through the post a special card known as a shuttle card; 'rating' the claim or deciding the appropriate rate of benefit by reference to the claimant's age, sex, dependants and contribution record; 'computing' the claim or calculating the amount of benefit payable by reference to the rate of benefit and the number of days for which it is payable and preparing the postal draft which constitutes the means of payment.

Under the moving belt system an officer may spend his whole time on one process relating to one type of benefit. This concentration on what may be a small part of a lengthy process seems to lead to staleness and loss of interest. Moreover, as each officer may have to deal with only one type of claim, it is more difficult for him to deal at need with other benefits when, for example, a colleague is away sick. Under the other system groups will deal with related types of benefit, for example one group will take sickness, maternity and industrial injury claims, and will gain a high standard of skill in dealing with them. Another real advantage of the group system seems to be that when a small number of people is responsible for seeing claims through from start to finish the members of the group take a more personal interest in their clients and this leads to better handling of claims. Moreover, as the group has ready access to the records needed to decide claims, the movement of papers within the office is reduced to a minimum; this is an important consideration in regard to claims to sickness or injury benefit where speed is essential. The standard pattern for a local office favours the group system but in practice there are some variations. Some of the processes, postal draft writing for example, are often concentrated in the hands of one or two officers outside the groups, and variations are also necessary on account of inconvenient premises, especially where an office occupies an ordinary house and small rooms on several floors make it hard to organize the work on a uniform plan; in the very small offices there is little scope for elaborate organization.

Work connected with the payment of contributions is concentrated in a special section which deals with the exchange of cards, with all correspondence connected with missing cards and the non-payment of contributions and with applications for exemption from the obligation to pay contributions on grounds of low income. The Inspectors in charge of 'non-compliance' work operate from this section and it also arranges the sickness and other visiting work carried out from the office.

That the public appreciates the services afforded by local offices is shown by the number of people who call at them. In the six months following the Appointed Day there were over $12\frac{1}{2}$ million callers and they still number nearly half a million a week. Dealing with callers' questions is a very important part of the work of local offices and undoubtedly it is a great help to the public to be able to discuss their problems orally with officers of the Department, as many callers would find it difficult to put such complicated questions into writing.

There are also a small number of local war pensions offices which deal only with war pensions work: these are referred to in more detail in Chapter X.

SCOTLAND, WALES AND THE ENGLISH REGIONS

The functions of the Controllers in Edinburgh and Cardiff and of the ten English regions are essentially managerial. It is on the Controllers that responsibility rests for keeping the local office machinery running smoothly. A chart showing the organization of a typical regional office is given on page 149. The work is divided between three main branches, dealing respectively with the staffing and supervision of local offices: the collection of contributions, including much of the preliminary work connected with prosecutions for non-payment of contributions: and the organization and general working of the machinery for deciding claims to benefit, including the working of the local appeal tribunals, the medical boards and the medical appeal tribunal used for deciding medical questions arising on claims to industrial injury benefits; but not war pensions medical boards which are arranged and supervised from Blackpool.

To assist him in carrying out this work the Controller has a Deputy and two or more Assistant Regional Controllers, each of whom is in charge of a particular branch of the work, with the necessary supporting staff. There is also a medical staff under a Senior Medical Officer who reports direct to the Chief Medical Officer at Head-quarters on medical matters and a Regional Finance Officer who is responsible to the Accountant-General.

The Regional Finance Officer makes all necessary arrangements with the Post Office and the banks for the supply of funds needed to pay benefits and pensions, such wages as are paid in cash locally and other disbursements. He also directs the internal audit of local offices under the direct control of the Accountant-General at Head-quarters. Local offices are audited twice a year and the audit is a very thorough one. It is a great tribute to the way in which the auditors do their work that, in spite of the inevitable dislocation in the rhythm of the office and the no less inevitable conflicts between the points of view of those concerned mainly with financial rectitude and those who place service to the public first, auditors are welcomed by the managers who have come to rely on them to draw their attention to things they may have overlooked in the running of their offices.

In addition to the internal audit a regular survey of offices is carried out under the supervision of the Controller. Regional survey is concerned with the general efficiency of the office as a whole rather than with results measured in pounds, shillings and pence. Survey, again, is to be distinguished from the work done by teams that may be sent down to local offices by the O. & M. Division at headquarters. Broadly speaking survey is concerned with the way existing instructions are being carried out in the individual office; O. & M. are looking to see whether the general instructions about organization need altering to get greater efficiency. It is sometimes said that local offices are visited too often by too many people for too many different reasons, but it is difficult to see how they could have been brought to their present state of efficiency if they had been allowed to develop each in its own way without close supervision and guidance.

The Controller is specially concerned with the well-being and morale of the staff in the region. Each region has a Whitley Council on which local matters are discussed and there are extensive staff welfare and recreational arrangements. In the realm of sport there is plenty of healthy rivalry between regions and a number of trophies are competed for annually. Questions concerning premises for local offices used to occupy a great deal of time when the Ministry was first set up. Premises were hard to find and many offices were housed in unsuitable buildings, especially in areas that had suffered heavy damage from air raids. The re-housing of local offices has proceeded steadily and has called for close co-operation with the regional organization of the Ministry of Works. The general standard is now fairly good but there are still too many offices in private houses that do not lend themselves readily to efficient organization, however pleasant they may be on amenity grounds, and some of them are very pleasant indeed.

There is close and constant contact between the regional staffs and headquarters, especially on establishment and allied matters, and senior officers from the regions are kept in touch with the way things are going by frequent conferences at headquarters. Since the two Ministries were amalgamated regional offices have taken over responsibility for the war pensions offices and local pensions offices in their regions and also for arrangements for the Local War Pensions Committees the functions of which are described in Chapter III.

HEADQUARTERS

The headquarters staff deals with all matters of general and financial policy and with all the Department's Parliamentary business; it includes the heads of the professional and technical branches. The general arrangement of the work at headquarters is shown in the chart on page 147.

Questions of policy affecting matters for which the Department is responsible fall into two groups. There is the all-important, and constantly recurring, question of the general level of rates of benefit, pensions and contributions; there is also a stream of smaller questions affecting particular types of benefit and the rules or conditions for paying them. Policy does not, however, enter into the decision in individual cases. In this respect the work of the Ministry differs sharply from the work of a Department such as the Ministry of Housing and Local Government which is constantly called upon to decide individual cases on grounds of policy alone, whether, for example, to allow a new scheme of development to proceed or to approve the design of some important building. The benefits and pensions paid by the Ministry of Pensions and National Insurance are payable as of right, subject to the fulfilment of the statutory conditions, and policy cannot be urged as a ground for making a payment to a person who does not fulfil them or withholding payment from one who does.

Alterations in the main pension and benefit rates involve the expenditure of such large sums that they are inevitably matters for the Government as a whole; a shilling on the main rates, with corresponding changes in subsidiary rates, for example, adds about £16 million to the immediate cost. Increases in the insurance pension and benefit rates also involve increases in contributions of such amount as the Government Actuary advises would be appropriate in order to preserve the general insurance basis of the scheme.

Alterations in individual benefits are usually put forward with the idea of removing anomalies or defects in the existing rules rather than as a deliberate attempt to improve them on grounds of broad policy. Questions affecting particular rules or conditions for national insurance or industrial injury pensions or benefits, but not the rates at which they are to be paid, are often referred to the National Insurance Advisory Committee or the Industrial Injuries Advisory Council for advice before any final decision is taken on them. The conditions for maternity benefits, for example, were altered in 1953 following a general review which was originally undertaken with the object of finding a better way of spending the money then available for these benefits. The functions of these two bodies are described later in this chapter.

The collection of the necessary material to enable decisions to be reached on these and similar policy questions and to prepare legislation and regulations required to give effect to Ministerial decisions and the day-to-day discussions with other Government Departments on matters of common interest, make up the main functions of the headquarters divisions. They also deal with questions arising out of Ministerial correspondence, Parliamentary Questions and other Parliamentary business.

In addition to the ordinary financial work of preparing estimates and appropriation accounts, the Accountant-General has to deal with questions connected with the two insurance funds, the National Insurance Fund and the National Insurance (Industrial Injuries) Fund, and with matters arising out of the internal audit of local offices.

Staff matters and matters relating to the organization of the Department come within the province of the Director of Establishments and Organization. The size of the staff, the varied sources from which it has been recruited and the way it is distributed over the country all add considerably to his responsibilities. The urgency attending the launching of the new schemes made it necessary to invent many new procedures and to put them into operation 'straight off the drawing board' without the opportunity of testing them on a small scale beforehand; with the not unnatural result that a good deal of revision has been necessary. There is a strong Organization and Methods Division under the Director of Establishments and Organization. In the early days this reported on major matters direct to a committee consisting of all the senior administrative staff under the chairmanship of the Permanent Secretary. This arrangement proved to be specially valuable when the plans were being made for the new Ministry, as it enabled decisions to be reached quickly.

THE MEDICAL SERVICES

The general arrangement of the Medical Department of the Ministry, which comprises 168 doctors under a Chief Medical Officer, is shown in the chart on page 151. Most of its work is connected with the medical boards and appeal tribunals which assess disability for war pensions and industrial injury disablement pensions. It is responsible for securing the doctors needed to man the boards; but members of the medical staff of the Department do not sit on medical boards other than the special boards that deal with claims arising out of pneumoconiosis and byssinosis. With the help of lay staff the medical staff prepare the case papers and where necessary obtain specialist's reports for the use of boards sitting to assess claimants' injuries. In war pensions cases they advise the Minister on the medical aspects of a claim and in industrial injury cases they scrutinize the decisions of medical boards to see that they are broadly in line with similar cases decided elsewhere and, if not, consider whether a reference should be made to a medical appeal tribunal. Most of the war pensions work is done at Blackpool. Industrial injury cases are dealt with in the regions where the medical staff, as is commonly the case with technical staff, are in direct contact with the Chief Medical Officer and his senior colleagues at headquarters on medical matters.

The senior medical staff in London, in addition to supervising the work of the doctors in Blackpool and in the regions, maintain contact with the Medical Departments of other Ministries, especially with those of the Health Departments and of Ministry of Labour and National Service, also with the Medical Research Council and the Medical Schools of the Universities. There are also contacts with the British Medical Association especially on the all-important question of medical certification on which the proper administration of sickness benefit so largely depends. One section specializes in matters relating to industrial diseases. They advise on individual claims to benefit and make it their business to keep in touch with developments in industrial medicine and especially with developments which might suggest that another disease should be added to the list of industrial diseases under the Industrial Injuries Act. Their knowledge and experience is at the disposal of the committee of the Industrial Injuries Advisory Council which advises the Minister on these questions.

SOLICITOR'S DEPARTMENT

The legal staff of the Ministry consists of a Solicitor and fifty professional officers who work in London. There are no lawyers attached to the regional staffs but arrangements are made for providing the Controller in Scotland with any legal advice and assistance he may require on matters of Scottish law.

Members of the legal staff are responsible for advising on all legal matters arising in the course of administration. They are responsible for drawing up instructions to Parliamentary Counsel to prepare any legislation that may be needed to carry out Government decisions. They draft alterations in the Royal Warrants for war pensions and any new regulations needed to give effect to alterations in the conditions governing the payment of pensions or benefits, and they conduct prosecutions for offences against the Acts and Regulations and civil proceedings in the County Courts, mostly for the recovery of arrears of contributions. They also conduct proceedings in the High Court in which the Ministry is involved—most of which are connected with war pensions. The Solicitor to the Ministry is also the Solicitor to the National Assistance Board.

THE STATISTICAL SECTION

The setting up, under a central authority, of comprehensive schemes of benefit for sickness and industrial injuries appeared to offer great opportunities for the production of statistical information about the incidence of different kinds of sickness and injury in different occupations; matters on which very little was known. At the outset consultations took place with doctors and others interested in these questions and steps were taken to collect the necessary data. It was not long before it became clear that the value of any statistics would depend on two factors over which the Department had no control. For information about the occupation of a claimant to sickness benefit the Department had to rely on the claimant himself or frequently on his wife if he was too ill to fill in the claim form. It was found that all too often this information was either missing or, if given, was in such vague terms that it could not be used for statistical purposes. For the nature of the illness, another essential factor, the Department was dependent on the doctor who gave the medical certificate. Here too it was found that, sometimes because doctors were unwilling to disclose to the patient the real nature of his illness, but more often owing to the pressure under which they were working, especially in times of epidemic, many certificates were given in such general terms as to be of little use as a basis on which to compile elaborate statistical tables.

It was eventually decided to collate and publish the information given in the medical certificates themselves and initially at any rate to make no attempt, so far as ordinary sickness was concerned, to construct tables showing the amount of sickness in different occupations. In 1951 some analysis for the most common diseases and broad occupational groups was attempted and further analysis on these lines may prove to be practicable.

For industrial injuries it has been possible to do rather more. When a claim to industrial injury benefit is received it is always referred to the employer for confirmation of the alleged injury. It has been possible in this way to obtain more accurate information about the man's occupation and industry and on the basis of this information tables have been prepared and published in the Ministry's Annual Reports showing the distribution of types of injury in various industries and some information has been given by industries about numbers subject to risk. In the absence of reliable information about the total numbers subject to risk in each occupation it has not been possible to show rates of injury in the various occupations.

There is plenty of information in the Ministry's records but it is by no means easy to make it available to the public in a form which will be useful. The field is almost too large as some 7 million claims to sickness benefit alone are made every year and experience has shown that the best method of producing useful statistics is to base them on a standing sample of the insured population. Although the information provided by statistics based on medical certificates is limited, medical authorities have expressed their appreciation of the indications given by the Ministry's figures about the general incidence of disease, many of which have been made available for the first time. In addition, research workers interested in a particular form of disease have, as the result of special enquiries made at their request, been given detailed information of considerable value. It may well be that it is by means of specialized enquiries of this kind that the greatest value can be extracted from the wealth of information regarding sickness and injuries contained in the Ministry's records.

The officer in charge of the Ministry's statistical work is in London but the machines used for preparing the cards and carrying out the other processes in the preparation of statistics are at Newcastle under the immediate control of a fully qualified statistician.

NEWCASTLE

The Ministry's office at Long Benton near Newcastle upon Tyne is the largest purely clerical establishment in the country and indeed in Europe. It has been visited by people from all over the world who have been favourably impressed by the arrangements for handling the enormous number of enquiries and records that have to be dealt with every day in the normal course of running our national insurance system. It covers 64 acres and consists of 16 blocks of single-storey buildings, some of which are connected by covered corridors; the longest corridor being over a quarter of a mile long. The decision to site this office at Newcastle followed the general policy of removing as much of the work of government as possible away from London and of securing 'a balanced industrial development in areas which, in the past, have been unduly dependent on industries specially vulnerable to unemployment'. With a payroll of over 6,500 the Ministry makes an important contribution to maintaining a steady level of employment in the district.

This large aggregation of staff created a number of unusual problems to solve which special measures were needed. The housing problems have been mentioned elsewhere. To provide transport for the staff a new station was built on the railway from Newcastle to the coast and a special service of buses that arrive at and depart from the offices on a strict time schedule had to be arranged. To enable this to be done without disrupting the normal bus services the Ministry adopted office hours that differ from those commonly worked in the neighbourhood. There is a special Post Office on the site and two large canteens where over 2,000 meals are served daily, as well as a small cafeteria for light meals in each of the 16 blocks.

Staff welfare and recreational facilities are well developed and rest rooms and first-aid facilities are provided. Teams from Newcastle have made their mark in more than one of the general civil service sports competitions.

The organizational problem at Newcastle is essentially the efficient handling of large numbers of small units of work and large numbers are the order of the day. There are 30 million record sheets to be kept up to date; 15 million queries from local offices are handled every year; indexes with over 40 million names have to be maintained and about 11 million order books containing over 500 million orders are issued each year. In order to secure the greatest possible measure of economy in such large-scale operations, much of the work is mechanized and experiments are continually going on with new methods and machines including the latest electronic devices.

A chart showing the general layout of the work at Newcastle is given on page 152. The work of the Family Allowances, Central Pensions, Statistics and Contributions Branches has already been described in connection with the services to which they relate and we shall deal here only with the Records Branch, which is a general service, and with the work of the Establishments and Organization Division.

Records Branch

A separate ledger account is kept for every insured contributor containing details of all the contributions paid by or in respect of him. There are some 100,000 ledgers each containing 300 sheets or about 30 million sheets in all; this figure includes a number of accounts which are dormant in the sense that for one reason or another the people to which they relate are not for the time being paying any contributions. These sheets are compiled mainly from the personal contribution cards which are called in every year in exchange for new cards, but an increasing number of contributions are being paid by the other methods described in Chapter VII and these must also be credited to the proper account. It is to spread this work evenly through the year that contributors have been divided into four groups with contribution years starting at different times of the calendar year. In addition to posting contributions actually paid, those deemed to have been paid or 'credited' must also be posted and to enable this to be done each local office sends up a form showing the number of contributions credited to each contributor during the year. Credited contributions relate in the main to periods when the contributor was drawing benefit and the Newcastle records do not record awards of short-term benefits like sickness or unemployment; details of these are recorded in the local office.

H

The posting of the ledgers naturally reveals a certain number of deficiencies and special notices have to be prepared and sent out to contributors who appear to have paid less than the full number of contributions due, though, as explained in Chapter VII, by no means every missing contribution is eventually found to be payable.

These elaborate records are kept partly as a check on the payment of contributions and partly because practically all the benefits under the main scheme are so linked with the payment of contributions that it is essential to know how a man's account stands when he claims benefit. A claim to benefit is made either at a local office of the Ministry or at an Employment Exchange and the information they need to deal with the claim is kept at Newcastle. Special arrangements had therefore to be made to enable the required information to be made available where it was wanted as quickly as possible. There is a batch of teleprinters linked with the regional offices available in an emergency, but the normal course is to use punched cards prepared in the local office and sent to Newcastle for completion and return to the office of origin; for rather obvious reasons these cards are called 'shuttle cards'. The flow of cards varies from 150,000 a week in the summer to something approaching 400,000 to 500,000 a week in the winter 'during an epidemic. About 10 million are handled every year. On receipt of a card from the local office it has to be matched with the appropriate ledger sheet, completed by the addition of the required information and returned to the sender, and the aim (which is generally achieved) is to get it back within three days. The ledger sheets are kept in numerical order based on the contributor's national insurance number and as a batch of cards from a local office will contain cards relating to contributors whose accounts are in a number of widely separated ledgers, the first step is to sort the cards under their respective ledger numbers. They are then conveyed to the appropriate ledger section by means of a vast system of pneumatic tubes which runs throughout the office blocks containing the Records Branch. The ledger clerk looks up the information in the ledger and enters it on the card which is then returned to a central point, where the cards are re-sorted into bundles for the various local offices; all this sorting is done mechanically. To maintain an efficient service of shuttle cards the Ministry rely heavily on the Post Office and special arrangements have to be made with the local Post Office authorities for handling the traffic it creates. The possibility of a breakdown in the long-distance postal services, for example owing to a railway strike, is one of the chances against which plans have to be prepared.

If the claimant gives his national insurance number his account can be identified easily and without delay, and fortunately most people do give their numbers. If the number is not given or is misquoted resort must be had to the Alphabetical Index which contains some 35 million separate slips. To trace a person in this index full Christian names and date of birth are needed, as there are so many identical surnames. There are, for instance, over 500,000 Smiths, so that a certain degree of despondency on the part of the staff is understandable when they are asked to trace 'Mary Smith' date of birth unknown and present address doubtful.

The Establishment and Organization Division

With a staff of over 6,500 and many complicated processes to control, the establishments and organization division at Newcastle has plenty to do. There is a separate Whitley Council for the office where many questions of local importance have been discussed and hammered out, especially in the early days when housing and other accommodation difficulties were very much in everyone's mind. The division possesses a large measure of autonomy, though naturally it works in close contact with London on all matters of general importance. The Controller is responsible for the procedures used at Newcastle and for the recruitment of staff locally.

There is a large proportion of young women on the staff and the turnover has been high. During the first ten years of working over 13,000 temporary clerks and other grades have been recruited in the area. Such a large turnover has meant that special attention has had to be given to training and a strong staff training branch has been kept fully employed. In the early days managers of local offices were inclined to be critical of the service provided for them by Newcastle, especially if delays in dealing with 'shuttle cards' lead to delays in the payment of benefit. Arrangements were accordingly made for managers to pay visits to Newcastle to see for themselves how the work was organized. These visits have provided an important link between two sides of an organization that might, if care had not been taken to avoid it, have developed a certain degree of antagonism towards each other.

Newcastle, like so much else in the Ministry, had to be brought into operation from scratch and with little experience to guide those responsible for planning it. When it started there were very few experienced clerks available and the work had to be broken down into the simplest possible processes and serialized to enable it to be done by a largely untrained staff. With experience and the skill that experience brings with it, it has been possible to rearrange the work in such a way that it can be done by fewer but higher-grade staff. In civil service terms the movement has been away from sub-clerical towards clerical work. In this way the staff has been reduced from nearly 9,000 to its present figure of about 6,500. But much of the work is still necessarily of a repetitive character and it is a tribute both to the management and to the qualities of the Novacastrian that, when a detailed investigation was made by a team working under Professor Bartlett of Cambridge, little or no trace was found of any fatigue or of loss of efficiency arising from the character of the work.

BLACKPOOL

The Blackpool Central Office which deals with war pensions is described in Chapter III.

THE MINISTRY'S STAFF

When the Ministry of Pensions and the Ministry of National Insurance were amalgamated two-thirds of the staff of the old Ministry of Pensions joined the new Ministry, and about a third, employed on work connected with medical treatment and the provision of artificial limbs and similar appliances, went over to the Ministry of Health.

The original staff for the Ministry of National Insurance was collected from many sources. About 5,500, of which 3,500 were temporary staff recruited during the war, were transferred from the Departments that had administered the old schemes of national health insurance, contributory pensions, unemployment insurance and workmen's compensation when the responsibility for these schemes was taken over by the new Ministry. By the end of 1945 the staff had risen to nearly 8,000, two-thirds of whom were temporaries.

In 1946 provision had to be made for the new family allowance scheme. There was only a small nucleus of established officers drawn from other branches of the Ministry and including a number of volunteers from other Departments and most of the staff had to be recruited in and around Tyneside on a temporary basis. Temporary staff were again needed in substantial numbers to cope with the work of raising pension rates and by the end of 1946 the staff had increased to 13,000, of whom over 70 per cent. were temporary.

In 1947 the big task of recruiting staff in readiness for the introduction of the new schemes began. They came from four main sources: the Approved Societies which were about to be wound up; other Government Departments whose work was likely to tail off with the end of the war; public assistance staffs of Local Authorities and normal recruitment into the civil service. Special selection boards on which Approved Societies and trade unions were represented, were set up by the Civil Service Commission to deal with applications for permanent posts from people outside the civil service; people seeking temporary posts were interviewed by boards set up by the Ministry itself. There were about 50,000 applicants of whom about 30,000 were interviewed; 12,500 were given permanent posts of whom 4,750 came from the Approved Societies, 2,500 from a miscellaneous field that included many people who had experience of workmen's compensation, 1,500 from Public Assistance staffs and 3,500 from other Government Departments and in addition a number of candidates were offered and accepted temporary posts. By the Appointed Day, 5th July, 1948, the total staff of the Ministry amounted to nearly 34,000 of whom just over half were temporary.

The permanent staff of the Ministry is organized in the recognized Treasury grades and there are no departmental grades such as are to be found in the Ministry of Labour and National Service. The recruitment of staff from so many different sources, many of whom had their own conditions of service and expectations, therefore raised some difficult problems of assimilation. Members of Approved Society staffs had rights protecting them against loss of employment or any reduction in remuneration following the winding up of the societies. To deal with these problems a special committee was set up on which the Approved Societies were strongly represented; the recommendations of this committee were unanimous and, with modifications on matters of detail, were accepted and put into operation by the Ministry in settling the new recruits into the civil service.

Very few of the new staff had any experience of the kind of work that would be expected of them in the new Ministry and from the outset great attention was given to staff training. Not only was it necessary to train the staff in the principles and practice of the new schemes, steps had also to be taken to ensure that those whose work would bring them into contact with the public were fully alive to the importance of a helpful and sympathetic attitude and knew how to conduct interviews. By the end of 1948 over 32,000 had passed through the training courses. Training did not stop after this initial effort: it has always been maintained at a high level. Most of it is now done in the regions and at the big central offices rather than at Headquarters, but for some years a headquarters training establishment has been maintained in London, mainly for instructing the more senior officers in the art or science of management.

The number of staff reached its highest figure of 39,650 in September, 1948; by January, 1957, it had fallen to 36,428 notwithstanding the amalgamation with the Ministry of Pensions in September, 1953, and the addition in October, 1954, of substantial extra work in connection with the distribution of welfare foods and cheap milk. When the two Ministries were amalgamated the combined staffs amounted to about 37,800, and it is estimated that the amalgamation resulted in a saving of about 800.

These reductions in staff have been made possible by improvements in office organization and methods of doing the work and by the skill and experience the staff have acquired through training and practical experience, and they have been achieved in spite of the fact that the work of the Ministry has steadily increased with the increase in the number of the insured population and by agency work undertaken by local offices for other Departments.

ADVISORY COMMITTEES

The National Committees

The committees which deal with war pensions have already been described in Chapter III and we shall deal here with the National Insurance Advisory Committee and the Industrial Injuries Advisory Council, to which brief reference has already been made, and with the local advisory committees.

These committees are statutory; the two central committees deal respectively with general matters affecting the national insurance and industrial injuries schemes as a whole and the local committees with matters of local interest.

The National Insurance Advisory Committee consists of a chairman and eight members appointed by the Minister, four of whom are appointed after consultation with employers' organizations, the Trades Union Congress, the friendly societies and the Government of Northern Ireland respectively. The committee exists to advise the Minister on any question relating to the operation of the Act that the Minister may choose to refer to it, including questions as to the advisability of amending the Act. Unlike the Statutory Committee set up under the Unemployment Insurance Acts, often known as the Beveridge Committee from the name of its first chairman, the National Insurance Advisory Committee has no responsibility for the finances of the scheme, the duty of reporting on them having been placed by the Act on the Government Actuary. A number of questions have been referred to the committee and several of its reports, all of which have been published, have formed the basis of amendments to the Act. In the early days the chief function of the committee was in connection with the making of regulations, the procedure for which is laid down in considerable detail in the Act. Before the Minister makes any regulations he must, unless he certifies that on account of urgency it is essential to make them forthwith, submit a draft to the committee for advice. Notice is thereupon given in the Press that the committee has regulations dealing with a particular topic before it and where copies of the regulations can be obtained and a period of 14 to 28 days is allowed for anyone affected by the proposals to send in objections and suggestions for modifications. The committee hears oral representations in support of objections and senior members of the staff of the Department also attend before the committee and explain the purpose of the regulations and the reasons for making them. The committee's report is published and has to be laid before Parliament with any regulations which the Minister, after considering the report, may make. These reports often contain suggestions for amending draft regulations originally submitted and these suggestions are almost always accepted by the Minister; if a Minister rejects the advice of the committee he must explain his reasons for doing so to Parliament.

The Industrial Injuries Advisory Council carries out similar duties in relation to the industrial injuries scheme. It is a larger body and rather differently constituted. It consists of a chairman and 15 other members appointed by the Minister; the only statutory requirement about membership is that it must include equal numbers appointed after consultation with organizations representing employers and workers respectively. Regulations about industrial injury matters have to be submitted in draft to the council, except in cases of urgency, but the procedure is not laid down in the same detail as in the National Insurance Act and their practice differs from the other committee. The council being a larger and more representative body, does not normally hear evidence, except through its special sub-committee which deals with industrial diseases, but obtains information about the views of those interested through its members, who consult the bodies at whose instance they were appointed. Officers of the Department attend the council and explain the intentions and reasons for the regulations. The reports of the council on draft regulations are seldom published and there is no obligation to lay them before Parliament.

It is difficult to say how far these differences in method and procedure were deliberate and how far the accidental result of two separate pieces of legislation. National insurance regulations tend to affect more people than industrial injury regulations and they are especially likely to affect sections of the public which are not organized in the same way as the workers most liable to industrial accidents and this, coupled with the Home Office tradition of consultation with both sides of industry in connection with workmen's compensation, may account for a good deal of the difference.

The Industrial Injuries Advisory Council has another important function. It is responsible for investigating diseases which it is thought may be industrial in origin with a view to their being added to the list of industrial diseases prescribed for the purposes of the industrial injury scheme. The Dale Committee (Cmd. 7557) had proposed that a special committee should be set up for this purpose but it was felt that it would be better to entrust the work to the Industrial Injuries Advisory Council, partly because it is a very responsible body representing the interests most affected but also because regulations might have to be made to add fresh industrial diseases and if there were two committees dealing with the same subject-matter there might be conflicts between them. The council has carried out a number of investigations and two diseases have been added in consequence. This work is done by a sub-committee of the council; this device was adopted to make it easier to co-opt specialists in particular diseases that are for the time being under consideration. The reports of the sub-committee are considered by the council as a whole before being sent to the Minister and they have all been published.

These two committees have not only been of the utmost value to the Ministry in administering the Acts, they also illustrate a device of government of which greater use might well be made in other fields. The procedure whereby the merits of and reasons for proposed regulations are explained by civil servants to an independent but well-informed committee whose reports are then made public seems to be a good answer to critics who complain that regulations are too often made behind closed doors by civil servants who are under no compulsion to explain their motives, and there is no doubt that the necessity for going through this procedure is a very wholesome discipline for the Department itself.

The first chairman of the National Insurance Advisory Committee was Sir Will Spens, one time Master of Corpus Christi College, Cambridge, who held office from 1946 until December, 1956, when he was succeeded by Sir Ifor Evans. Sir Wilfrid Garrett was chairman of the Industrial Injuries Advisory Council from 1947 to 1954; he was succeeded by Sir Arnold Plant. A great tribute is due to the part the chairmen played in guiding the committee and the council during the difficult and sometimes hectic days when the vast mass of regulations required to launch the two schemes was in course of preparation.

The Local Advisory Committees

Two hundred and thirty local advisory committees were set up under the National Insurance Act for the purpose of advising on questions bearing on the administration of the Act. They consist of some twenty people chosen by the Minister after consultation with various bodies representing insured contributors. In view of the methods used for deciding individual claims to benefit as described in Chapter VIII, local advisory committees have little scope for considering individual cases. They are, however, consulted on matters of local interest such as the opening or closing of local offices in their area, and in the early days of the scheme many of them gave valuable help in finding suitable premises for offices. As the administration has settled down it has inevitably happened that fewer questions arise on which their advice is needed. This is in itself a tribute to the way in which the Ministry carries out its work as there can be no doubt that if things started to go wrong in any locality the local committee would very quickly get to know about it and bring matters to the attention of the Department. National questions affecting the schemes as a whole do not fall within the province of the local committees but an exception was made in connection with the first quinquennial review of the national insurance scheme in 1954 when every local committee was specifically invited to put forward points which they thought should be considered; in response to this invitation a number of matters were brought to the notice of the Department.

There was originally no corresponding provision for local committees in the Industrial Injuries Act but members of the committees inevitably took a great interest in the working of that Act and from time to time expressed views about it. It was therefore arranged that, pending the formal extension of their functions to include industrial injury matters, any representations they cared to put forward informally about that scheme would receive full consideration. The functions of the committees were extended to cover industrial injury matters by an amendment of the Industrial Injuries Act in 1953.

The local committees usually meet once a quarter and they are provided with full and detailed reports about the administration of the Acts in their areas.

CHAPTER X

Reciprocity and International Agreements

*

AFTER the war social security came to be regarded as an important instrument of policy in international affairs. Among the Brussels Treaty Powers and in the Council of Europe attempts were made to hammer out an international system of social security and the International Labour Office produced a Convention laying down minimum standards for a satisfactory system for adoption by the member nations. There have also been international conferences on war pensions at which matters of common interest to disabled ex-service men were discussed. In these discussions representatives of the Ministry or of the Ministries that preceded it, took a leading part.

The social security needs and aspirations of individual nations vary so much that it proved difficult to work out any general scheme or to lay down satisfactory standards of general application. It was not easy to find the common factor between a nation that attaches most importance to stimulating the birth-rate by a generous system of family allowances and one that is haunted by memories of large-scale unemployment, or to balance a scheme that provides a generally acceptable level of benefits for practically the whole population against one that gives exceptionally high rates of benefit to a small proportion of the industrial workers.

More practical results have been obtained by bilateral and multilateral agreements between countries with similar social security schemes. Some countries, for example, make nationality a test for participation in social security plans. Great Britain does not impose this test and agreements have been made with countries that do under which citizens of the United Kingdom obtain the same treatment as is accorded to the nationals of the other party to the agreement. Other agreements have aimed at enabling the national of one country who goes to live in another country to take his social security rights with him. These agreements may, for example, provide that in qualifying for short-term benefits like unemployment benefit or sickness benefit, a migrant may count contributions paid under the social insurance scheme in his country of origin. Agreements on pensions have taken the form of mutual undertakings under which each country promises to pay a pensioner a proportion of the standard rate of its national pension based on the number of contributions paid in the country concerned. Agreements on these lines have been made with France, the Netherlands, Luxembourg, Italy and the Federal Republic of Germany and at the end of 1956 negotiations were in progress with Austria, Belgium and Yugoslavia. With countries like Sweden, whose pension schemes are not based on contributions, agreements have been made or are being sought along different lines; they may well take the form of providing for the payment of the whole pension at the national rate by the country in which the person concerned is living when he reaches pension age.

Agreements have also been made with Australia and New Zealand, neither of which has adopted our style of contributory pension. The agreements with these countries provide that for the purpose of rights in this country residence in the other country is treated as if the person concerned had lived here as an insured contributor and had duly paid all his contributions. An emigrant from this country will be paid pensions and other benefits under the local schemes on the same terms as people who have always resided in the country to which he goes. If a person who is already in receipt of a United Kingdom pension goes to live in one of these countries he will carry his pension with him and it will be made up by the country of his adoption to its current rate.

Northern Ireland and the Isle of Man have their own systems but they are practically identical with ours and agreements have been made with them under which contributions and benefits paid in one territory are treated exactly as though they had been paid in the other. The effect of these agreements is to produce what is practically a single system and a man who goes from one territory to the other can claim benefit or pension on the same terms as if he had remained at home. In the case of Northern Ireland a balancing payment is made from the National Insurance Fund so as to bring the finances of the two schemes into line.

These agreements require benefits and pensions to be paid in this country to people who have not complied with the contribution conditions laid down in the various Acts and to make this legally possible those Acts have had to be modified. The Acts contain provisions enabling this to be done by Order in Council so far as is necessary to give effect to the agreements, but as it would be a tedious, and indeed almost an impossible, task to go through all the Acts and modify them section by section whenever an agreement is made, the practice has grown up of scheduling the agreement to the Order in Council with a general clause declaring that the Acts and regulations are to be read subject to such modifications as are necessary to secure to anyone coming within the scope of the agreement, the rights provided for him.

A complete list of the reciprocal arrangements now operating is given in Appendix VII. Most of these agreements have been worked out at international conferences held in various parts of the world and the drafting of the agreement itself calls for great care and skill. The language used must be as simple and direct as possible so that it can be read by the ordinary reader who is not specially learned in social security law; terms of art employed only in the legislation of one country are for this reason avoided. On the other hand the agreement must be sufficiently precise to enable it to be interpreted by the statutory authorities who deal with claims to benefit in this country, should any question arise about the rights of any person claiming benefit or pension under the Order in Council to which it is scheduled.

CHAPTER XI

Conclusion

*

IT was in 1944 that a start was made with the social security plans foreshadowed in the Beveridge Report and the general provisions of the National Insurance and Industrial Injuries Acts did not come into operation until 1948. So it is much too soon to draw any conclusions about the impact of these schemes on the welfare of the community or about the organization set up to administer them. All one can attempt is to offer in the light of the experience gained so far, a few comments on the three main subjects described in the earlier chapters of this book: the general administrative arrangements of the Ministry; the special system of adjudication under which claims to pensions and benefits are decided; and the provisions of the schemes themselves.

GENERAL ADMINISTRATIVE ARRANGEMENTS

Most of the administrative machinery had to be set up 'straight from the drawing board'. Everyone was anxious to get the new schemes started at the earliest possible moment and there was no time to experiment with alternative plans. As a result there was perhaps a certain amount of 'over insurance' in the early days; but it is easy to be wise after the event. The new Department had to undergo some severe tests through epidemics, frequent changes in rates of contributions and benefits and other events that placed serious strains on the organization and, although it emerged success-fully, there were moments when there was not much margin to spare.

There has been some replanning of the details of the administration in the light of experience but no major changes in the general plan, and so far as one can see no major changes are likely in the immediate future. Experience and systematic training have brought greater skill and aptitude in dealing with the complicated processes involved in carrying out the Ministry's work and, as a result, it has been possible to reduce both the number of offices and the staff employed in them. No doubt there will always be pressure for further economies, but if these complicated schemes are to be properly administered there must be adequate supervision and sufficient financial checks. These are expensive in terms of administrative costs but lax administration would be even more costly and might bring the whole principle of national insurance into disrepute. Possible economies in staff must be weighed against loss of revenue through failure to secure compliance with the obligation to pay contributions and extra expense through the payment of benefit to people who do not comply with the appropriate conditions.

A number of mechanical and other devices are already installed at Newcastle and research and experiment is constantly going on in an endeavour to secure greater efficiency and economy by these means. But so long as the general idea of an administration based essentially on the local office holds good these things have their limitations. The introduction of a new machine at Newcastle may merely transfer work from the local office to the central office with no immediate saving in cost and indeed with the probability of greater error, if, for example, it means that requests for information from local offices are received at a central point in Newcastle and then have to be transcribed there for distribution to the appropriate section of the Records Branch. In a highly mechanized office, too, the possibility of breakdowns and of stoppages through the absence of a few key operators or maintenance men must always be a matter of anxiety for those responsible for the smooth running of the organization. With millions of people depending for their livelihood on the regular despatch of order books and of the information needed to enable local offices to pay benefits promptly economies in manpower might have to be paid for at too high a price.

No one with practical experience of these schemes would deny that local offices are essential if they are to work smoothly, but doubts have frequently been expressed whether so many offices are necessary and whether economies could not be secured by combining the Ministry's offices with those of other Departments. An experiment was made in 1953 to test the idea of combined offices to serve both the Ministry of Pensions and National Insurance and the Ministry of Labour and National Service.[1] From the offices of the two Departments which happened to be sharing premises 50 were chosen for the experiment, the staffs were combined and put under a single manager selected from one of the departments; 25 were put under managers from the Ministry of Labour and National Service and 25 under managers from the Ministry of Pensions and National Insurance. The two staffs were made interchangeable as far as possible and the combined office became a single administrative unit which carried out

[1] For a full account of this experiment see: H. Trevor Woolston, 'The Joint Local Office Experiment', *Public Administration*, Summer, 1955 (Vol. XXXIII, No. 2).

the full range of duties that each of the two offices separately had been doing; but the different types of work continued to be reported to the Ministry responsible for that work through its own channels and instructions to the local office regarding the work were transmitted in the same way. The experiment went on for about a year and was then abandoned. It produced little economy in staff over and above the economies which might have taken place during the period with separate offices. Indeed the combined office was frequently of such a size as to require a higher-grade officer to manage it, and this often offset economies in other directions. Perhaps the main lesson that has been learned from the experiment is that if local offices are properly staffed for the work they have to do amalgamation is only likely to lead to economies in staff if the work of the offices to be combined fluctuates in such a way that slack periods in one service coincide with heavy periods in the other so that the staff can be kept fully employed throughout the year. Amalgamation produces its own problems, especially in the sphere of management. The range of work in a combined office can be very wide indeed and may well be too wide for one man to supervise; this may mean higher-grade staff and it is easy to offset economies in this way. There may be savings in typing and other common services but if offices are housed in the same building these can be secured by pooling without combining the managerial duties. There are probably important savings to be made by housing the local offices of several Departments in one building and much has already been done in this direction but further progress may require an extensive building programme and will therefore have to wait.

Various ideas for grouping some or all of the work done in the Ministry's own local offices have also been tried. The general verdict on these experiments has been that the time and effort spent in sending papers and records from outlying offices to the central office of the group and back again outweighs savings in other directions. The mere fact that papers have to be sent from one office to another under such arrangements means that they are out of action for considerable periods and in times of stress this can cause serious delays.

The self-contained local office may not always be the most economical unit but it seems to be the best means of giving the public the kind of service it needs and is entitled to expect.

SYSTEM OF ADJUDICATION

In common with other administrative tribunals the arrangements for deciding claims to the various pensions and benefits administered by the Ministry came under the scrutiny of the Committee on Administrative Tribunals and Enquiries, whose report was published in July, 1957 (Cmnd. 218). The Committee said that the impression they had gained of the system as a whole was most favourable. They observed that it was generally considered to have operated smoothly for many years and they were satisfied that no structural changes were called for. This tribute to the men and women who, in all parts of the country, have devoted time and energy to the working of the local tribunals, which are the mainspring of the system, is well deserved. The system must inevitably seem complicated to anyone trying to comprehend it as a whole but in practice few members of the public are concerned with more than one aspect of it at a time and, for each separate pension or benefit, the line of appeal from the initial decision is fairly well sign-posted.

Among the points specially considered by the Committee was whether there should be an appeal from a decision of the National Insurance and Industrial Injuries Commissioners. This was a matter that had been the subject of special debate in the House of Lords while the Industrial Injuries Bill was going through Parliament and an amendment to create such an appeal was rejected. The Committee came to the conclusion that all decisions of tribunals should be subject to review by the Courts on points of law in some form or another and in general they thought that the best way to secure this was to have a straightforward appeal to the Courts on points of law. In the case of the National Insurance and Industrial Injuries Commissioners, however, they thought that special considerations arose. The status of the Commissioners, the fact that they could sit as a tribunal of three, the need for avoiding delay in reaching a final decision on a claim to benefit and the views of the T.U.C., who had expressed themselves as satisfied with the existing position, convinced the Committee that it would be right to make an exception and to leave any review by the Courts in these cases to be exercised by the special procedure of *certiorari*. They were also satisfied with the working of the pensions appeals tribunals and made no recommendations for substantial changes. They did, however, recommend that appeals in family allowance cases should in future be decided by local tribunals with an appeal to the Commissioner instead of by the special referees mentioned above on page 93. Apart from this the Committee had no alterations of structure to suggest and in the light of their recommendations and findings it is reasonable to assume that in principle the existing system will continue much as it is. The Committee made one general recommendation which, in its application to the services run by the Ministry, would have the effect of removing from the Minister most of the responsibility for the conduct of local tribunals. They proposed that two councils should be set up, one for England and Wales and one for Scotland, which would be responsible for supervising the procedure followed by the tribunals and also for the appointment of the members of the panels from which they are made up. The English council would be the responsibility of the Lord Chancellor and the Scottish council would come under the Secretary of State. Chairmen of tribunals would in future be appointed by the Lord Chancellor in England and in Scotland by the Lord Chancellor, Lord President of the Court of Session or the Lord Advocate as might be thought appropriate, instead of by the Minister. These recommendations, which apply to all tribunals, are designed to emphasize the independence of administrative tribunals from any appearance of ministerial control; though the Committee were at pains to make it clear that they had had no significant evidence that influence was in fact exercised on members of tribunals by Government Departments. They also made some detailed suggestions which, if adopted, would alter several of the procedural rules described in Chapter VIII.

They considered that the proceedings of the national insurance tribunals, like those of the industrial injuries tribunals, should be in public unless the chairman decides to hear a case in private on the ground that it will involve the disclosure of intimate personal or financial circumstances. They recommend that, again like the industrial injuries tribunals, legal representation should be allowed in national insurance cases with the leave of the chairman, but that leave should only be given where the chairman is satisfied that the claimant is in such a position that he cannot satisfactorily put his case unless he is allowed to employ a lawyer. They also recommend the abolition of limitations on the right of appeal from the local tribunal to the Commissioner, while retaining the right of the Commissioner to dispose of cases without an oral hearing if he thinks fit. These are important alterations in arrangements which have worked smoothly for many years and if they are adopted it will be interesting to watch their effect.

PROVISIONS OF SCHEMES

The questions which arise on any attempt to review the provisions of the various schemes of pensions and benefits administered by the Ministry are so largely political in character that it would be out of place to say much about them in a book of this kind.

The history of war pensions goes back to 1916. As far as one can see, the general shape of the present scheme as embodied in the various Royal Warrants and other instruments is accepted by the

I

organizations which speak for disabled men. The broad conception of a basic pension based on a medical assessment of the degree of disability caused by service in the forces, with special allowances for men who are prevented by their injuries from earning their living and for those suffering from specially serious and disabling injuries, seems to give general satisfaction, though there will always be pressure for larger pensions and for new kinds of allowances to meet special types of case. On the administrative side the main problem that has dogged the administration of war pensions, the difficulty of making suitable arrangements for a specialized service catering for a comparatively small group that may expand suddenly and then contract again to relatively modest proportions, has been solved by amalgamating it with the national insurance administration which serves the same people in different ways throughout the whole of their lives and which, by its very size, introduces the necessary stability into the administrative machine. There seems to be every reason to expect that the arrangements introduced with general approval in 1953 will continue to provide a satisfactory service for men and women disabled in the service of their country.

The industrial injuries scheme was completely new to industry. Workers were accustomed to a scheme under which they were compensated for loss of earning power following an industrial accident and the change to a scheme based on a medical assessment of the degree of disability brought with it some unexpected consequences which had to be modified by the introduction and subsequent enlargement of the special hardship allowance. Considering the extent of the changes made from the principles of the old workmen's compensation scheme the new arrangements met with very few difficulties in their early days, but it is too soon to say whether the scheme will now settle down or whether further changes will be found to be necessary.

The early years of the national insurance scheme were overshadowed by steadily rising prices and by the difficulty of adapting an insurance scheme providing pensions and benefits at fixed rates to the situation resulting from inflation. These difficulties were met by increasing the standard rate of pension and benefits when it fell too far behind the rising cost of living and it is difficult to see what else could be done within the general frame-work of the scheme. There has been so little unemployment that the unemployment provisions of the scheme have hardly been tested, but in relation to sickness benefit and pensions there are signs that public attention is for the time being turning to different methods of providing for people who through illness or old age are unable to earn their own living. It was always part of the broad Beveridge plan that, the national minimum having been provided through national insurance, steps should be taken in other ways to improve the lot of the sick and the old still further. Although no figures seem to be available there can be little doubt that the number of workers covered by arrangements under which their employers continue to pay wages during the first days and even weeks of sickness is increasing, and that in time these sick pay schemes will form an important element in the general provisions against illness. As regards old age, the report of the Committee on the Economic and Financial Problems of Provision for Old Age drew attention to the increasingly important part that is being played by occupational pensions schemes. They estimated that in 1954 some 7 million people or about one-third of the population contributing to the national insurance scheme were acquiring rights under some form of pensions scheme and that the number was steadily growing. More recently there have been references to supplementary pension schemes on a national scale. Many difficult questions will arise in working out these further schemes and it would be unprofitable to speculate on what form they will ultimately take, how they will affect the existing schemes and what part the Ministry will play in their administration.

Although, therefore, it seems that the national insurance schemes introduced in 1948 will not be the nation's last word on the provision against want, they provide the essential foundations on which any further developments in this important element of the Welfare State will be built and in the laying of those foundations the Ministry can claim to have played a notable part.

List of the Main Rates[1] of War Pensions and Allowances current during June, 1957

		Weekly rate	
		s.	d.
1. Disablement			
Pension	100 per cent.	85	0
allowance for wife	100 per cent.	10	0
allowance for each child	100 per cent.	7	6
Supplementary Allowances (payable in certain cases in addition to the pension):			
unemployability supplement		55	0
constant attendance allowance[2]	up to	35	0
allowance for lowered standard of occupation	up to	34	0
comforts allowance[3]		10	0
	or	20	0
age allowance	between 5s. and	15	0
additional treatment allowance[4]	up to	50	0
allowance for wear and tear of clothing— up to £6 or £10 per annum			
education allowance for children— up to £80 per annum for each child			
Allowances for wife and child (replacing those shown above) payable with unemployability supplement and treatment allowances:			
allowance for wife		30	0
or			
allowance for adult dependant		30	0
allowance for first or only child		15	0
2. Death Pensions			
Widow's pension[5]		66	0
	or	20	0
allowance for each child		25	0
rent allowance	up to	25	0
education allowances for children— up to £80 per annum for each child			
Widower's pension (if incapable of self-support and in need)	up to	66	0
Orphans:			
under 15 years		30	0
15 years and over		40	0
over 18 and incapacitated		50	0

NOTES

1. The pension rates shown are for ex-privates and equivalent ranks. Higher rates are payable to officers and non-commissioned officers and to their widows.

2. Exceptionally, in cases of very severe disablement, the maximum weekly allowance is 70s.

3. The higher rate is payable to pensioners receiving both the unemployability supplement and constant attendance allowance, and to certain other severely disabled pensioners.

4. A pensioner receiving treatment approved by the Ministry and which treatment prevents him from working receives in place of his pension an allowance equal to a pension at the 100 per cent. disablement rate. In certain circumstances a pensioner who is not entitled to sickness benefit or retirement pension may be granted an additional allowance of 50s.

5. The higher rate is payable to widows who have children eligible for an allowance, or who are over 40, or who are incapable of self-support.

Pensions and Benefits provided under the National Insurance Acts, 1946 to 1957

1. The National Insurance Acts provide cash benefits, generally in return for contributions, for the main circumstances causing the interruption or cessation of earnings, and to help to meet the expenses of a birth or death in the family. The benefits are:

> Unemployment benefit,
> Sickness benefit,
> Maternity benefits—
> > maternity grant,
> > home confinement grant,
> > maternity allowance,
> Guardian's allowance,
> Death grant,
> Widow's benefits—
> > widow's allowance,
> > widowed mother's allowance,
> > widow's pension,
> > widow's basic pension,
> Child's special allowance,
> Retirement pension.

The principal standard rates of benefit are the same.

2. There are generally two contribution tests; the first requires that a certain number of contributions shall have been actually paid at any time since entering insurance, and unless this condition is satisfied, no benefit is due; the second requires that a certain number of contributions shall have been paid or credited in respect of a specified period, and if this condition is not fully satisfied benefit may be paid at a reduced rate. Contributions are credited for weeks in respect of which benefits are paid (and in certain other circumstances) so that the misfortunes against which the national insurance scheme provides cover may not themselves cause deficiencies in the contribution record governing payments at a later date. The record for the whole period of insurance is taken into account in assessing the rate of a pension, but for short-term benefits such as those for unemployment and sickness it is the contribution year immediately preceding the current benefit year which governs the rate of benefit in that year: the benefit years are so arranged that they start five months after a contribution year has ended to allow time for the contributions paid to be recorded in the central accounts, and for any arrears due to be collected. There are time limits within which any such arrears must be paid.

3. Contributions must be in the class appropriate to the benefit claimed. Class I (employed contributors) covers all benefits; Class II (self-employed

contributors) covers all except unemployment benefit; and Class III (non-employed contributors) covers all benefits except those for unemployment and sickness and the maternity allowance. However, if certain conditions are satisfied, contributions of one class can sometimes be treated as if they were in another class, for the purpose of fixing the rate of a short-term benefit.

4. Insured persons with dependants may receive increased benefits: for example, an extra 30s. by way of unemployment or sickness benefit is provided for a wife, 15s. for the first child, with 7s. (over and above the family allowance of 8s. or 10s.) for each subsequent child. Where no increase is payable for a wife, a similar addition may be claimed for some other adult dependant who is a close relative and, in the case of a man, incapable of self-support, or for a woman who is looking after the claimant's child.

5. There are rules which generally prevent anyone from drawing more than one benefit at a time, or from drawing an increase of benefit for someone receiving personal benefit in his own right. These rules also usually prevent payment for the same contingency from two sources financed from public funds; for example, a man injured at work cannot draw injury benefit and sickness benefit together, and a widow cannot receive a widow's benefit under the general scheme as well as one under the industrial injuries scheme or a pension as a war widow. Following the same principle, the rate of benefit is reduced at the end of eight weeks if treatment as a hospital in-patient under the National Health Service, which provides maintenance as well as treatment free of charge, continues longer than that time; if it continues longer than a year a resettlement sum may be payable on discharge.

6. Benefits are not in general paid in respect of periods of imprisonment or detention in legal custody.

7. National insurance benefits may or may not be payable to an insured person who is outside Great Britain, for example sickness benefit is payable only if the absence abroad is temporary and is for the purpose of receiving treatment for an illness which commenced in this country. Some benefits are payable only in countries with which there is a reciprocal arrangement; in some cases the national insurance contributions give title, under reciprocal agreements, to the corresponding pensions and benefits of the country in which the insured person is staying; and in some cases benefit is payable, but at the rate payable when the pensioner left Great Britain, that is, without the benefit of any additions subsequently given because of increases in the cost of living in this country.

8. Claims must be made within time limits which vary for different benefits. For example, sickness must be notified in writing to the Ministry's local office within three days of its onset, and benefit must be claimed within ten days, but these periods can be extended if there is good cause for delay and a person making his first claim to sickness benefit since 1948 is allowed 21 days. The actual time limit applicable to the benefit depends on the need to ensure that all the conditions are satisfied—not always easy, in respect of a past period—and to safeguard against massive late claims, remembering that the object of the benefits is generally to provide a means of current maintenance. There are similarly time limits on the encashment of most postal drafts and orders issued in settlement of claims.

9. Provisions specific to the different benefits are outlined below.

UNEMPLOYMENT BENEFIT

Standard weekly rates

Single person	50s.
Married woman	34s.
Man and wife	80s.
Man, wife and two children	102s.
Boy or girl under age 18 without dependants	28s. 6d.

10. Unemployment benefit may be paid, provided the contribution conditions are satisfied, to unemployed people under age 70 (65 for a woman) who are capable of work and available for further employment. Men between 65 and 70 and women between 60 and 65 are entitled to unemployment benefit only if they have not retired and if, in addition to satisfying the usual conditions, they would be eligible for a retirement pension if they had retired. Benefit is payable on a daily basis for each day of the week except Sunday. But it cannot be paid for any day for which wages are received (apart from earnings of not more than 6s. 8d. a day from a spare time job) or for which a claimant receives compensation for loss of remuneration which together with the single person's rate of benefit amounts to more than two-thirds of his previous earnings. Benefit is not payable during holidays, except in certain circumstances where workers have been compelled to take an unpaid extra holiday in addition to their normal one. Benefit may be withheld for a period of up to six weeks in the case of those who:

(1) leave employment without just cause or lose it through misconduct; or
(2) refuse a suitable job or (in appropriate cases) training, when offered; or
(3) neglect to take advantage of a reasonable opportunity of suitable employment or training.

'Suitability' is determined individually by reference to previous experience, training, employment record, the length of time a man has been out of work and his chance of finding work in his regular occupation in the district. In the case of a man who has been out of work a long time the work offered might be less well paid than his last job, but it must not be paid at a rate which is lower than those generally given under trade union agreements or, failing such agreements, those generally recognized by good employers.

11. Benefit is not payable if employment has been lost by reason of a stoppage of work due to a trade dispute, so long as the stoppage of work continues, unless neither the man nor any of his fellow workmen at his place of employment and in the same grade or class are participating in, financing or indirectly interested in, the dispute. A job made vacant by a trade dispute is never regarded as 'suitable employment' for the purpose of the disqualifications described in the last paragraph.

12. The contribution conditions are:

First—That at least 26 contributions in Class I (i.e. as an employed person) have been paid; and

Second—That at least 50 Class I contributions have been paid or credited (e.g. for weeks of sickness or unemployment) in the contribution year which governs benefit at that time; a reduced rate of benefit is payable if less than 50 but at least 26 contributions are recorded.

Widows who have just ceased to be entitled to widow's benefit otherwise than on re-marriage are given special concessions to re-establish them in insurance.

13. The first three days of unemployment are normally 'waiting days' and are paid only if there are at least 12 such days or days of sickness incapacity in a period of 13 weeks from the first 'waiting day' of either. Isolated days off work separated by a week or more from any other such day are ignored altogether.

14. Benefit is payable in the first instance for a basic period of up to 180 days, not counting Sundays, but may be continued up to a maximum of 492 days, the number of days depending on the record of contributions paid and benefit drawn. Once benefit has been exhausted, no more can be paid until a further 13 contributions have been paid in respect of employment.

15. There are special conditions for the payment of unemployment benefit to share fishermen and seasonal workers, and for people who do not ordinarily work on every day in the week.

16. Unemployment benefit is generally paid in cash at an Employment Exchange of the Ministry of Labour and National Service but is sent by post to persons who live more than six miles from an Exchange.

SICKNESS BENEFIT

Standard weekly rates

Single person	50s.
Married woman	34s.
Man and wife	80s.
Man, wife and two children	102s.
Boy or girl under age 18 without dependants	28s. 6d.

17. Sickness benefit is payable, provided contribution conditions are satisfied, to insured persons under age 70 (65 for women) and not yet retired, who are incapable of work 'by reason of some specific disease or bodily or mental disablement', or excluded from work by a local Medical Officer of Health because they are carriers of, or have been in contact with, an infectious illness. Receipt of salary, wages or sick pay from an employer or from some other source does not affect title to benefit. A claimant may be disqualified for receiving benefit for up to six weeks, however, if the incapacity is the result of his own misconduct or if, without good cause, he fails to undergo medical examination when required to do so, indulges in behaviour likely to retard his recovery, leaves his residence without leaving word where he may be found, or does any remunerative work other than work from which his earnings are not more than 20s. a week, undertaken under medical supervision as part of his treatment in hospital or in some similar institution. The amount of sickness benefit payable to an insured person aged between 65 and 70 (man) or 60 and 65 (woman) is limited by the amount of pension payable if retirement were notified; and there are special conditions governing benefit for mariners and airmen, married women, widows and, exceptionally, persons abroad.

18. The contribution conditions are:

First—That at least 26 contributions in Class I or Class II (i.e. as an employed or self-employed person) have been paid; and

Second—That at least 50 Class I or Class II contributions have been paid or credited (e.g. for weeks of sickness or unemployment) in the contribution year which governs benefit at that time; a reduced rate of benefit is payable if less than 50 but at least 26 such contributions are recorded.

Widows who have just ceased to be entitled to a widow's benefit otherwise than on re-marriage are given special concessions to re-establish them in insurance.

19. There are rules about 'waiting days' as for unemployment benefit and, similarly, isolated days off work are disregarded.

20. Benefit is payable for up to 312 days if less than 156 contributions in Class I or Class II have been actually paid; if 156 or more such contributions have been paid, it can continue indefinitely (this test is regarded as satisfied by those who paid at least 104 contributions under the National Health Insurance scheme or who have paid 156 contributions partly under one and partly under the other scheme).

MATERNITY BENEFITS

Standard benefits

Maternity grant	£12 10s.
Home confinement grant	£5
Maternity allowance	50s. a week

(Where the conditions are satisfied, all three may be paid for one confinement.)

21. The *maternity grant* is a lump sum paid before or after a confinement to help with the general expense of having a baby. It can be paid on the mother's own insurance, or on that of her husband, but not on both. For multiple births, additional grants can be paid up to the number of newly born children still living 12 hours after birth. No grant is normally payable for a still birth, but one grant may be paid for a still birth if the pregnancy has lasted at least 28 weeks. The contribution conditions are:

First—That at least 26 contributions of any class have been paid for the period between entering insurance and the date, or expected date, of confinement; and

Second—That at least 26 contributions of any class have been paid or credited (for example, for weeks of sickness or unemployment) for the contribution year which governs benefit at the time when the confinement takes place or is expected.

These contribution conditions need not be satisfied, if those for a maternity allowance (see below) are fulfilled.

22. The *home confinement grant* is a lump sum paid to help to meet the extra expenses where the baby is born elsewhere than in hospital accommodation provided at public cost (and in a few cases of emergency removal to hospital if the stay is short). Not more than one grant can be paid for each confinement. There are no separate contribution conditions; provided a maternity grant is payable the home confinement grant can be paid too in appropriate cases.

23. The *maternity allowance* is a weekly payment of 50s. (if the contribution conditions are satisfied) and is payable from 11 weeks before the expected week of confinement for 18 weeks or, if the baby is late, until six weeks after the week in which it is born. The allowance is not payable for any week in which remunerative work is undertaken. The contribution conditions, which must be satisfied by the mother, are:

First—That not less than 26 contributions in Class I or Class II (i.e. as an employed or self-employed person) have been paid in the 52 weeks ending 13 weeks before the expected week of confinement; and

Second—That at least 50 Class I or Class II contributions have been paid or credited for the same 52 weeks.

No allowance is payable if the first condition is not satisfied, but if the first condition is satisfied but there are less than 50 contributions paid or credited in the period, a reduced rate of allowance is payable.

24. Increases for dependants can be paid, as for sickness and unemployment benefit.

GUARDIAN'S ALLOWANCE

Standard rate 27s. 6d. a week

25. A guardian's allowance is payable in respect of an insured person's child who is left an orphan. It is paid to the person in whose 'family' (within the definition given to that word in the Family Allowances Act) the child is included after the death of the parents—usually the person maintaining the child. If there is more than one child, an allowance is payable for each of them, whether they are with the same or different guardians. For a child in a home or institution an allowance can be paid only to someone outside the home who is contributing to the child's maintenance.

26. An adopted child can attract an allowance on the death of his adoptive parents (but the allowance cannot be paid to his natural parents); conversely, no allowance can be paid for an adopted child while his adoptive parents are still living.

27. In a few cases an allowance can be paid on the death of one parent: where the paternity of an illegitimate child has not been established, where the parents are divorced and the surviving parent did not have the custody of the child and was not maintaining it, or where the other parent cannot be traced.

28. A guardian's allowance is payable only while the child is under the age limits. A child is under these age limits:

(1) Up to the normal school-leaving age (15); and
(2) For any further period before his eighteenth birthday while he:
    (*a*) is receiving full-time instruction in a school or is an apprentice, or
    (*b*) would still be a schoolchild or apprentice but for ill health.

An apprentice for this purpose means a young person undergoing full-time training for any trade, business, profession, etc., and not earning enough substantially to provide a livelihood.

29. There are no contribution conditions for guardian's allowance.

DEATH GRANT

Standard grant for a person aged 18 *or over who was on* 5*th July*, 1948

Aged under 55 (50 for a woman)	£25
Aged 55 but less than 65 (man) or 50 but less than 60 (woman) }	£12 10s.

Standard grant for a child

Under 3 years	£7 10s.
3 to 5 years (inclusive)	£12 10s.
6 to 17 years (inclusive)	£18 15s.

30. Death grant is a single payment made (if contribution conditions are fulfilled) to help to meet the expenses connected with the death of an insured

man, his wife, child or widow; or of an insured woman, her husband, child or widower. Payment cannot be made in respect of the death of a man or woman who on 5th July, 1948, had reached the minimum retirement pension age (65 for a man, 60 for a woman), or for a child under the age of 10 who was born before that date; there is no payment for a still-born child.

Until recently the person claiming the death grant was required to show that he had certain specified expenses to meet in connection with the death. The National Insurance Act, 1957, however, provided for the grant to become simply a payment on death and for it to be paid under regulations as if it were a benefit due to the deceased at his death.

32. The contribution conditions are:

First—At least 26 contributions of any class must have been paid or credited since 5th July 1948; and

Second—At least 45 contributions must have been paid or credited in the last complete contribution year before the date on which the conditions have to be satisfied.

No grant is payable unless the first condition is satisfied but if the second condition is not satisfied there is an alternative test. If an average of at least 45 contributions a year has been paid or credited over the whole period of insurance from 5th July, 1948 (or the sixteenth birthday, if later), the full grant can be paid; if this average is less than 45 but not less than 13, a reduced grant is payable.

33. For the death of an adult the contribution conditions may be satisfied by the deceased insured person himself or by his spouse (whether still living or not). For the death of a child they may be satisfied by a parent, a person in whose family the child was at the time of death, or by a deceased person in whose family the child was when that person died.

WIDOW'S BENEFIT

Standard weekly rates

Widow without children

widow's allowance (first 13 weeks)	70s.
widow's pension	50s.
widow's basic pension	10s.

Widowed mother	one child	two children	three children
widow's allowance (first 13 weeks)	90s.	102s.	114s.
widowed mother's allowance	70s.	82s.	94s.

34. Widow's benefits are paid, subject to satisfaction of the contribution conditions, to the widows of insured persons, the type of benefit depending on the age of the widow and her circumstances—whether she has children or is looking after adolescent sons or daughters who have just started earning their living. The benefit is payable until the conditions on which it is paid cease to be satisfied, or until the widow re-marries. It is not payable for any period during which a widow is cohabiting with a man as his wife.

35. The contribution conditions, which must be satisfied by the deceased husband, apply equally to all kinds of widow's benefit and are—

First—That 156 contributions of any class have been paid since entry into insurance (contributions towards widow's pension insurance under the

Widows', Orphans' and Old Age Pensions Acts are taken into account, and in certain cases of contributors under these Acts 104 contributions are sufficient); and

Second—That an average of at least 50 contributions have been paid or credited for each complete year of insurance (calculated from 1936 in the case of those who last entered insurance earlier) up to the date of his death, or, if earlier, the date on which he reached the minimum pension age (normally 65).

If the first condition is not satisfied, no benefit is payable. If the first condition is satisfied but the contribution average is below 50 but not below 13, benefit is payable but at a reduced rate.

36. *Widow's allowance* is payable for 13 weeks. The normal rate is 70s. a week and a widowed mother receives an additional 20s. for her first child and 12s. for each subsequent child (additional to the family allowance in payment for them). Widow's allowance is payable irrespective of the age of the widow, unless her husband had already qualified for his retirement pension before death. It is not affected by earnings.

37. If when the widow's allowance finishes there is a qualifying child in the widow's family, she receives *widowed mother's allowance* until such time as her children have grown up or otherwise left her family. The allowance comprises a personal benefit of 50s. with 20s. for the first and 12s. for each subsequent child.

38. For a widow to qualify for the allowance, she must have in her 'family' as defined in the Family Allowances Act either a son or daughter of the deceased husband or a child who was in his 'family' or able to be treated as being in his family, when he died. The amount payable for a child or children continues up to the ages applicable to allowances under the Family Allowances Act (the eighteenth birthday, if still at school or an apprentice; otherwise the date of leaving school or finishing apprenticeship, if earlier). So long as at least one child remains under the age of 18 and is living with his mother, her personal allowance can continue even though the child may already be earning his living. A widow who is expecting a child by her late husband receives this personal allowance until the baby is born, when the full rate becomes payable.

39. The personal element in a widowed mother's allowance is subject to reduction if she herself takes up work and earns more than 60s. a week; the reduction is 6d. for every shilling earned between 60s.–80s. and 1s. for every shilling earned in excess of that amount. The amounts paid in respect of her children are not affected.

40. A *widow's pension*, normally 50s. a week, is payable after the widow's allowance to a woman widowed between the ages of 50 and 60 who had been married at least three years, and to a widowed mother whose entitlement to widowed mother's allowance ceases while she is between those ages, provided it is then at least three years since her marriage. In certain cases women who have been married more than once can have the duration of the marriage linked for the purpose of satisfying this test.

41. A widow's pension used to be paid until the age of 60 was reached and was then converted automatically into a retirement pension at the same rate. The National Insurance Act, 1957, made the widow's pension continue until retirement or age 65 and provided for her then to qualify, with the aid of her husband's contribution record for the period of the marriage, for retirement pension on her own insurance. This was done to enable the widow who works after age 60 and does not draw her pension to pay contributions and earn increments in the rate of her retirement pension.

42. Between 1948 and 1956 a woman who when she ceased to be otherwise entitled to widow's benefit was incapable of self-support by reason of some infirmity and likely to continue to be so incapable for a prolonged period could be awarded a widow's pension irrespective of her age, and this pension continued to be payable so long as she remained incapable of self-support by reason of that infirmity. Some of these pensions remain in payment but no new awards have been made since 7th January, 1957. Widows are now re-established in insurance if and when their widow's benefit ceases otherwise than on re-marriage so that they can become entitled to full sickness benefit if at that time they are sick, or to full unemployment benefit if fit but unable to find a regular job.

43. A widow's earnings affect her pension. The rule is the same as that applicable to retirement pensioners.

44. A *widow's basic pension* is a transitional right, preserved only for widows who were married before 5th July, 1948, and whose husbands were insured under the Contributory Pensions Acts immediately before that date. The pension is payable only if no other widow's benefit is in payment at a higher rate; but underlying entitlement can serve to prevent a widowed mother's allowance or widow's pension from being reduced below 10s. on account of earnings.

RETIREMENT PENSION

Standard weekly rates

	Pension from minimum qualifying age (65 for men, 60 for women)	Maximum rate—retirement deferred to age 70 (65 for women)
Single person	50s.	65s.
Married couple—		
wife not insured	80s.	105s.
wife insured	100s.	130s.

45. Retirement pension is payable, subject to contribution conditions, to people who have reached the minimum pension age, 65 for a man or 60 for a woman, and have retired from regular employment, or who have reached age 70 for a man or 65 for a woman irrespective of whether or not they are still at work. Until July, 1958, there is a special requirement that insurance must have lasted at least ten years.

46. A retirement pensioner can claim an increase of benefit (30s.) for a dependent wife under age 60, and increases for any children in his family. A married woman can have her own pension of 30s. on her husband's insurance when he qualifies for his pension, if she has reached age 60 and is herself retired, but a woman who marries after age 60 cannot qualify for pension on her husband's insurance until three years after the date of her marriage, unless on marrying she lost a widow's benefit under the National Insurance scheme or some other pension from public funds.

47. On widowhood a wife's retirement pension is increased to the single person's rate. A woman widowed after age 60 whose husband was not receiving a retirement pension can receive widow's allowance for 13 weeks, and afterwards a retirement pension at the single person's rate.

48. Retirement from regular employment does not necessarily mean giving up work altogether; a person can be treated as retired although he is engaged in a gainful occupation provided that his work is not inconsistent with retirement, for

example if it is done only occasionally or is inconsiderable in extent. However, if a pensioner under the age of 70 (65 for a woman) works, a limit is set to what he can earn without his pension being affected. Where earnings exceed 50s. a week pension is reduced by 6d. for every 1s. earned between 50s. and 70s. and by 1s. for every 1s. earned in excess of 70s. a week.

49. People who do not retire at the minimum pension age and continue at work can earn higher pensions when they do retire or reach age 70 (65). The pension is increased by 1s. 6d. a week for every 25 contributions paid for weeks of work after age 65 (60) and up to 70 (65). A wife's pension on her husband's insurance is increased by 1s. for every 25 contributions paid by him after both he and she have passed the minimum pension age. If she is widowed she receives an extra 1s. 6d. on her widow's retirement pension replacing each additional 1s. her husband has earned for her. Regulations made under the National Insurance Act, 1957, enable retirement pensioners, other than married women with pensions on their husbands' insurance, to de-retire and to earn increases by payment of contributions for weeks of work.

50. The contribution conditions for a retirement pension are:

First—That at least 156 contributions have been actually paid between the date of entry into insurance and the date on which age 65 (60 for women) is reached (for those whose last entry into insurance was before 30th September, 1946, 104 paid contributions are sufficient); and

Second—That an average of at least 50 contributions have been paid or credited for each complete year of pensions insurance up to age 65 (60 for women); a reduced rate of pension is payable if average is less than 50 but at least 13 such contributions. The average is calculated from the date of last entry into insurance, or 1936 if later, or (for many years to come) 1948, if earlier.

A married woman can draw a pension either on her own insurance or on that of her husband, but not on both. There is an additional condition before she can qualify on her own insurance—that contributions have been paid or credited for at least half the weeks in the period between the date of her marriage and reaching pensionable age (with a slightly modified test for those who married before 5th July, 1948). A widow claiming pension on her own insurance is deemed to satisfy the first contribution condition if she was entitled to a widow's allowance following her husband's death, and she can use her husband's contribution record for the years before his death to help her to satisfy the second condition.

CHILD'S SPECIAL ALLOWANCE

Standard weekly rate

One child 20s.; each additional child 12s.

Since 18th November, 1957, a woman whose marriage ended in divorce and whose former husband has since died can claim an allowance for her children. Contribution and other conditions are similar to those for widow's benefit, but payment is limited to the amount contributed by the husband in his lifetime towards the cost of providing for the children.

List of the Main Rates[1] of Industrial Injuries Pensions and Allowances provided under the National Insurance (Industrial Injuries) Acts, 1946 *to* 1957

	Weekly rate	
	s.	d.
1. *Industrial Disablement*		
Injury Benefit[2]	85	0
increase for wife or other adult dependant	30	0
increase for first child	15	0
increase for each other child	7	0
Disablement benefit[3]: pension for disablement assessed at 100 per cent.	85	0
Supplementary allowances with disablement benefit		
unemployability supplement[4]	50	0
constant attendance allowance[5] up to	35	0
special hardship allowance up to	34	0
2. *Industrial Death Benefit*		
Widow's pension (first 13 weeks of widowhood)	70	0
Widow's pension[6,7]	56	0
or	20	0
Widower's pension (if incapable of self-support)	56	0

NOTES

1. Lower rates are in general paid to boys and girls under 18.

2. Payable for incapacity for work due to industrial accident or disease within the 'injury benefit period', i.e. up to a maximum of 26 weeks from the date of the accident or development of the disease.

3. Disablement benefit is paid if a person is still suffering a loss of faculty as a result of the accident or disease when the 'injury benefit period' ends.

4. Where an unemployability supplement is in payment, increases may be paid for dependants as for injury benefit.

5. Exceptionally, in cases of very severe disablement, the maximum weekly allowance is 70s.

6. Increases are payable for children, if any, as for injury benefit, but at a rate 5s. higher for each child.

7. The lower rate is payable to childless women widowed under age 50, unless over 40 on ceasing to be entitled to an allowance for a child or for the care of a young person.

Special Schemes for Persons Injured before 5th July, 1948

The schemes described below are designed to help certain people injured at work by accident or disease before the National Insurance (Industrial Injuries) Act, 1946, came into force. They either supplement payments of workmen's compensation or provide an allowance in cases where no compensation is payable under the Workmen's Compensation Acts.

All the allowances mentioned below are payable out of the Industrial Injuries Fund. The provisions of the different schemes are dovetailed in with those of the Workmen's Compensation Acts and the Industrial Injuries Acts. The rules governing claims and payments, for example, are generally similar to those applying to claims for industrial injuries benefits.

WORKMEN'S COMPENSATION (SUPPLEMENTATION) SCHEME, 1951

This Scheme made under the Workmen's Compensation (Supplementation) Act, 1951, and operating from 11th July of that year covers persons injured before 1st January, 1924, in receipt of, or with an underlying right to, weekly payments of workmen's compensation. It is designed to put them into broadly the same position as persons injured after that date to whom the later Workmen's Compensation Acts applied. In particular it provides for a review of the compensation payable where there has been an increase in wage rates of the pre-accident employment, and brings the maximum compensation payable up to 40s. a week.

The amount of the allowance is such sum as will bring the total weekly amount payable by way of workmen's compensation and supplement:

(a) In the case of a man who is totally incapable of work to 40s.; and
(b) In the case of a man who is partially incapacitated, to two-thirds the loss of earnings suffered as a result of the accident subject to a maximum of 40s.

The loss of earnings is assessed by comparing the current earnings of people doing the job in which the man was engaged before his accident with the amount the man is able to earn at the present time. The Scheme is administered by the Workmen's Compensation Supplementation Board. The Board has a centralized staff in London but also receives help from the Ministry's local offices in making any necessary enquiries.

From the commencement of the Scheme the number of allowances awarded up to December, 1956, totalled 3,400 of which 2,430 were still in force at that date.

THE PNEUMOCONIOSIS AND BYSSINOSIS BENEFIT SCHEME, 1952
(AS AMENDED)

The Pneumoconiosis and Byssinosis Benefit Scheme which came into operation on 10th March, 1952, was made under the Pneumoconiosis and Byssinosis Benefit Act, 1951. At first it covered only persons totally disabled by pneumoconiosis or byssinosis and the dependants of persons dying from these diseases, but from 10th November, 1954, it was extended by the Pneumoconiosis and Byssinosis Benefit Amendment Scheme, 1954 (made under the Pneumoconiosis

K   145

and Byssinosis Benefit Act, 1951, as extended by the Industrial Diseases (Benefit) Act, 1954), to cover persons who were only partially disabled.

Allowances under the Scheme are payable in cases where there is no title to payments under the Workmen's Compensation Acts or under the Industrial Injuries Acts. A weekly allowance of 40s. is payable to totally disabled persons. Supplements in respect of unemployability and constant attendance, and increases for dependants can also be awarded on the same terms as to disablement pensioners under the Industrial Injuries Act. The allowance for partial disablement is at the rate of 20s. a week.

In the case of a death due to pneumoconiosis or byssinosis, members of the deceased's family who were wholly or in part dependent on his earnings at the time of his death (or would have been so dependent but for his disablement) are entitled to a sum not exceeding £300.

The Scheme is administered by the Pneumoconiosis and Byssinosis Benefit Board which operates in the same way as the Workmen's Compensation Supplementation Board.

From the commencement of the Scheme the number of allowances awarded has been as follows:

	Awards	Allowances in force at 31st December, 1956
Total disablement	4,574	2,700
Partial disablement	5,980	5,307
Deaths	2,045	–

INDUSTRIAL DISEASES (MISCELLANEOUS) BENEFIT SCHEME, 1954

This Scheme, made under the Industrial Diseases (Benefit) Acts, 1951 and 1954, makes provision, corresponding to that described above in relation to pneumoconiosis or byssinosis, for people suffering from certain forms of occupational skin cancer and certain conditions resulting from excessive exposure to X-rays or radio-active substances. It came into force on 8th November, 1954.

The Scheme is administered by the Pneumoconiosis and Byssinosis Benefit Board. Since its inception, awards have been as follows:

	Awards	Allowances in force at 31st December, 1956
Total disablement	5	2
Partial disablement	10	8
Deaths	9	–

THE WORKMEN'S COMPENSATION AND BENEFIT (SUPPLEMENTATION) ACT, 1956

This Act provides a supplement for totally disabled people who are still entitled or have since 5th July, 1956, been entitled to workmen's compensation or similar payments. Broadly it covers persons who are incapable of work as a result of the injury and likely to remain so incapable for at least thirteen weeks. Separate provisions apply to persons suffering from pneumoconiosis and byssinosis and to persons entitled to allowances for total disablement under the Pneumoconiosis and Byssinosis Benefit Scheme and the Industrial Diseases (Miscellaneous) Benefit Scheme: in general the supplement is payable if a certificate of total disablement has been issued. The supplement is at a flat rate of 17s. 6d. a week and became payable after 28th August, 1956. It is administered by the Ministry of Pensions and National Insurance largely through its network of local offices. Up to the end of 1956, 9,040 awards were made, of which about 8,800 were still current at the end of the year.

Chart 1—Organization of the Ministry

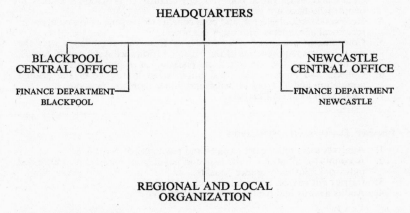

HEADQUARTERS

BLACKPOOL
CENTRAL OFFICE

FINANCE DEPARTMENT
BLACKPOOL

NEWCASTLE
CENTRAL OFFICE

FINANCE DEPARTMENT
NEWCASTLE

REGIONAL AND LOCAL
ORGANIZATION

HEADQUARTERS

1. *Office of the Minister.*
2. *Administrative Departments*—advise on the formation of policy and the preparation of legislation; direct the application of policy laid down by the Minister and Parliament.
3. *Establishments and Organization Department*—general staffing policy, organization and methods, procedural instructions, training, accommodation, information services and public relations.
4. *Finance Department*—financial control including procedural safeguards and audit; estimates; accounts.
5. *Legal Department*—advises on legal questions; instructs Parliamentary Counsel on legislative requirements; drafts statutory instruments; conducts enquiries; takes proceedings.
6. *Medical Department*—advises on medical questions; directs work of Medical Officers in Blackpool Central Office and the Regions; advises on questions connected with research.

BLACKPOOL CENTRAL OFFICE

1. Awards war pensions.
2. Maintains ledger accounts and index of war pensioners.
3. Issues and renews order books.
4. Arranges the hearing of appeals.
5. Maintains statistics of war pensions.
6. Deals with local staff matters.

FINANCE DEPARTMENT, BLACKPOOL

1. Audits awards and payments of war pensions and allowances.
2. Prepares estimates and accounts for War Pensions Vote.

NEWCASTLE CENTRAL OFFICE

1. Awards family allowances; maintains ledger accounts and alphabetical index for all families receiving allowances; issues and renews order books.
2. Maintains contribution accounts and alphabetical index of population insured for national insurance benefits and provides local offices with details needed to determine claims.
3. Maintains ledger accounts of retirement and widow pensioners; registers claims and issues order books; keeps records of provisional awards to people who have not yet retired.
4. Receives contributions for, and pays benefits to, persons overseas; operates reciprocal agreements with other countries.
5. Co-ordinates prosecutions work arising from non-compliance with the contributions requirements of the National Insurance Acts, benefit frauds, stamp manipulation and fraudulent encashment of postal drafts.
6. Collects and analyses statistical information in respect of the insured population and all types of beneficiary other than war pensioners.
7. Deals with local staff matters.

FINANCE DEPARTMENT, NEWCASTLE

1. Analyses local office cash receipts and payments of benefits.
2. Accounts for all postal drafts issued in payment of national insurance and industrial injuries insurance benefits.
3. Carries out payroll and related work.
4. Audits awards and payments of long-term benefits.

REGIONAL AND LOCAL ORGANIZATION

1. Central Offices for Scotland and Wales, and Regional Offices for the 10 English Regions, guide and control the work of 900 local War Pensions and National Insurance Offices; organize work of appeal tribunals; appoint members of tribunals and advisory committees, and medical boards; deal with local staff matters; deal with Press enquiries; conduct certain prosecutions in magistrates' courts.
2. Regional medical staff—advise Regional Controllers on medical questions; arrange and scrutinize the work of medical boards and arrange the medical treatment of war pensioners.
3. Regional Finance Officers—fund local offices (with cash, postal drafts and order books) and arrange for the audit of their records.
4. War Pensions Offices—receive claims for pensions and allowances; arrange medical boards; award and pay certain allowances; look after the welfare of war pensioners with the help of War Pension Committees; supervise children in care of the Minister and other children for whom allowances are being paid.
5. National Insurance Offices—receive claims for family allowances and adjust order books in respect of unforeseen changes of circumstances after the books have been issued; receive claims for, and award all national insurance and industrial injuries insurance pensions and benefits except unemployment benefit; pay sickness benefit, industrial injury benefit, maternity benefits, widows' allowances and death grants; arrange for central payment of widows' and retirement pensions, disablement pensions and associated allowances, and industrial death benefits; adjust pension order books in respect of earnings or hospital in-patient treatment; advise enquirers on all questions of entitlement to benefits and liability for contributions; credit contributions for periods of incapacity for work; exchange national insurance contribution cards; check compliance in area with contributions requirements of the National Insurance Acts.

Chart 2—Organization of a Typical Regional Office

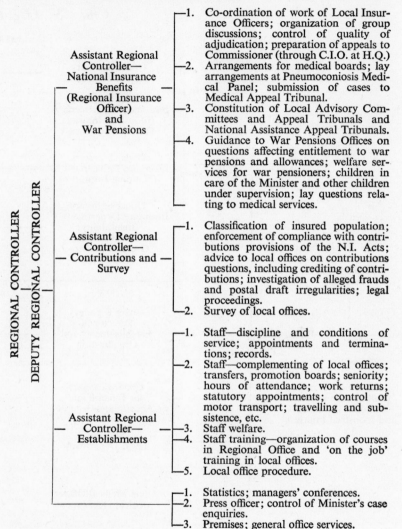

REGIONAL CONTROLLER | **DEPUTY REGIONAL CONTROLLER**

Assistant Regional Controller— National Insurance Benefits (Regional Insurance Officer) and War Pensions

1. Co-ordination of work of Local Insurance Officers; organization of group discussions; control of quality of adjudication; preparation of appeals to Commissioner (through C.I.O. at H.Q.)
2. Arrangements for medical boards; lay arrangements at Pneumoconiosis Medical Panel; submission of cases to Medical Appeal Tribunal.
3. Constitution of Local Advisory Committees and Appeal Tribunals and National Assistance Appeal Tribunals.
4. Guidance to War Pensions Offices on questions affecting entitlement to war pensions and allowances; welfare services for war pensioners; children in care of the Minister and other children under supervision; lay questions relating to medical services.

Assistant Regional Controller— Contributions and Survey

1. Classification of insured population; enforcement of compliance with contributions provisions of the N.I. Acts; advice to local offices on contributions questions, including crediting of contributions; investigation of alleged frauds and postal draft irregularities; legal proceedings.
2. Survey of local offices.

Assistant Regional Controller— Establishments

1. Staff—discipline and conditions of service; appointments and terminations; records.
2. Staff—complementing of local offices; transfers, promotion boards; seniority; hours of attendance; work returns; statutory appointments; control of motor transport; travelling and subsistence, etc.
3. Staff welfare.
4. Staff training—organization of courses in Regional Office and 'on the job' training in local offices.
5. Local office procedure.

1. Statistics; managers' conferences.
2. Press officer; control of Minister's case enquiries.
3. Premises; general office services.

Also stationed in Regional Office:

Regional Medical Officer and supporting medical staff (reports to Chief Medical Officer at Headquarters).
Regional Finance Officer and supporting staff (reports to Accountant-General at Headquarters).

Chart 3—Organi

(as at

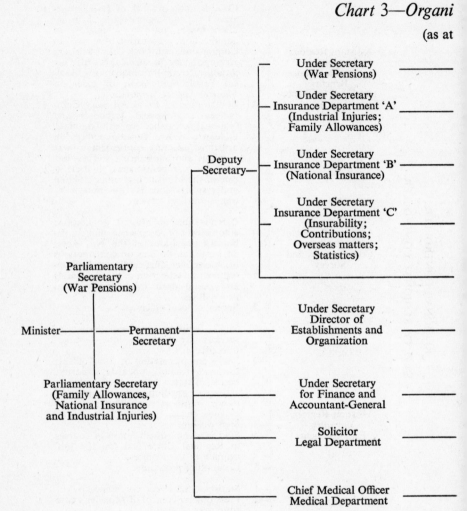

zation at Headquarters

January, 1958)

1. Policy and general questions on war pensions.
2. Rehabilitation and welfare.

1. Industrial injuries scheme (diseases); workmen's compensation.
2. Industrial injuries scheme (accidents and general questions).
3. Family allowances; guardians allowances; overlapping benefits; adjudication arrangements (family allowances and all national insurance benefits).

1. Unemployment benefit; widow's benefit; dependency questions (all national insurance benefits).
2. Retirement pensions; death grant.
3. Sickness and maternity benefits.

1. Collection of contributions.
2. Overseas agreements; international matters.
3. Statistics; general intelligence.
4. Insurability; classification; options; crediting of contributions.

Chief Insurance Officer—adjudication matters other than procedure.

1. Headquarters and Central Office matters; manpower; promotions; staff welfare.
2. Conditions of service; pay; staff movements; staff training; staff relations.
3. Regional and local office complements, organization, procedures; agency work.
4. Organization and methods; office services; instructions.
5. Public relations: press office and publications.

1. Administrative finance; finance and central accounts of the N.I. Funds.
2. Estimates; vote accounting; appropriation accounts.
3. Regional Finance Officers; audit; general finance and procedure.

1. National insurance; national assistance; family allowances.
2. Industrial injuries; war pensions; special schemes.
3. Civil and criminal proceedings; disclosure and privilege.

1. National insurance; medical certification; morbidity statistics.
2. Industrial diseases; research; pneumoconiosis medical panels.
3. Regional medical organization; medical boards; medical appeal tribunals; industrial accidents.
4. War pensions—1914–18 war claims.
5. War pensions—1939–45 war claims.

Chart 4—Organization of Newcastle Central Office

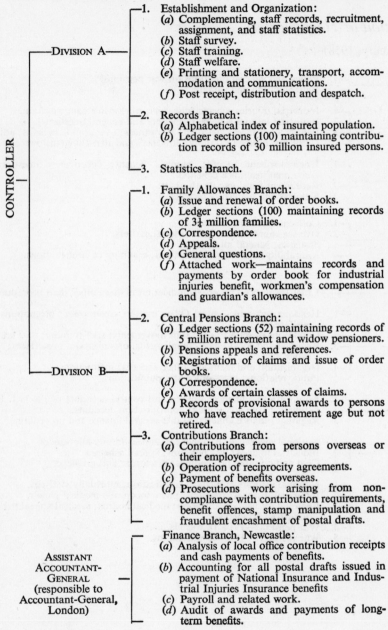

CONTROLLER

DIVISION A

1. Establishment and Organization:
   - (a) Complementing, staff records, recruitment, assignment, and staff statistics.
   - (b) Staff survey.
   - (c) Staff training.
   - (d) Staff welfare.
   - (e) Printing and stationery, transport, accommodation and communications.
   - (f) Post receipt, distribution and despatch.

2. Records Branch:
   - (a) Alphabetical index of insured population.
   - (b) Ledger sections (100) maintaining contribution records of 30 million insured persons.

3. Statistics Branch.

DIVISION B

1. Family Allowances Branch:
   - (a) Issue and renewal of order books.
   - (b) Ledger sections (100) maintaining records of $3\frac{1}{4}$ million families.
   - (c) Correspondence.
   - (d) Appeals.
   - (e) General questions.
   - (f) Attached work—maintains records and payments by order book for industrial injuries benefit, workmen's compensation and guardian's allowances.

2. Central Pensions Branch:
   - (a) Ledger sections (52) maintaining records of 5 million retirement and widow pensioners.
   - (b) Pensions appeals and references.
   - (c) Registration of claims and issue of order books.
   - (d) Correspondence.
   - (e) Awards of certain classes of claims.
   - (f) Records of provisional awards to persons who have reached retirement age but not retired.

3. Contributions Branch:
   - (a) Contributions from persons overseas or their employers.
   - (b) Operation of reciprocity agreements.
   - (c) Payment of benefits overseas.
   - (d) Prosecutions work arising from non-compliance with contribution requirements, benefit offences, stamp manipulation and fraudulent encashment of postal drafts.

ASSISTANT ACCOUNTANT-GENERAL (responsible to Accountant-General, London)

Finance Branch, Newcastle:
- (a) Analysis of local office contribution receipts and cash payments of benefits.
- (b) Accounting for all postal drafts issued in payment of National Insurance and Industrial Injuries Insurance benefits
- (c) Payroll and related work.
- (d) Audit of awards and payments of long-term benefits.

Ministers, Parliamentary Secretaries and Permanent Secretaries since 1944

MINISTRY OF PENSIONS

Ministers

Rt. Hon. Sir Walter Womersley (afterwards Sir Walter Womersley, Bart.).	(from 1939)
Rt. Hon. Wilfred Paling.	August, 1945
John Burns Hynd.	April, 1947
Rt. Hon. George Buchanan.	October, 1947
Rt. Hon. Hilary Marquand.	July, 1948
Rt. Hon. George Isaacs.	January, 1951
Derick Heathcoat Amory (afterwards The Rt. Hon. D. Heathcoat Amory).	November, 1951

Parliamentary Secretaries

Rt. Hon. Wilfred Paling.	(from 1941)
Captain The Hon. William Philip Sidney, V.C. (afterwards Viscount De L'Isle).	May, 1945
Jennie Laurel Adamson.	August, 1945
Arthur Blenkinsop.	May, 1946
Charles James Simmons.	February, 1949
Brigadier John George Smyth, V.C., M.C. (afterwards Brigadier Sir John Smyth, Bart.).	November, 1951

Permanent Secretaries

Sir Alexander Cunnison, K.B.E., C.B.	(from 1941)
Sir Harold Parker, K.B.E., C.B., M.C.	January, 1946
Sir Arton Wilson, K.B.E., C.B.	February, 1948

MINISTRY OF NATIONAL INSURANCE

Ministers

Rt. Hon. Sir William Jowitt, K.C. (afterwards Earl Jowitt).	November, 1944
Rt. Hon. Leslie Hore-Belisha (afterwards Lord Hore-Belisha).	May, 1945
Rt. Hon. James Griffiths.	August, 1945
Rt. Hon. Edith Summerskill.	March, 1950
Rt. Hon. Osbert Peake (afterwards Viscount Ingleby).	November, 1951

Parliamentary Secretaries

Charles Urie Peat, M.C.	May, 1945
George Samuel Lindgren.	August, 1945
Thomas Steele.	October, 1946
Harry Bernard Taylor.	March, 1950
Robert Hugh Turton, M.C. (afterwards The Rt. Hon. R. H. Turton).	November, 1951

153

Permanent Secretaries

Sir Thomas Phillips, G.B.E., K.C.B.	November, 1944
Sir Henry Hancock, K.C.B., K.B.E., C.M.G.	January, 1949
Sir Geoffrey Stuart King, K.C.B., K.B.E., M.C.	August, 1951

MINISTRY OF PENSIONS AND NATIONAL INSURANCE

Ministers

Rt. Hon. Osbert Peake (afterwards Viscount Ingleby).	August, 1953
Rt. Hon. John Boyd-Carpenter.	December, 1955

Joint Parliamentary Secretaries (War Pensions)

Brigadier John George Smyth, V.C., M.C. (afterwards Brigadier Sir John Smyth, Bart.).	August, 1953
The Hon. Richard Wood.	December, 1955

Joint Parliamentary Secretaries (National Insurance)

Robert Hugh Turton, M.C. (afterwards The Rt. Hon. R. H. Turton).	August, 1953
Ernest Marples (afterwards The Rt. Hon. Ernest Marples).	October, 1954
Edith Maud Pitt, O.B.E.	December, 1955

Permanent Secretaries

Sir Geoffrey Stuart King, K.C.B., K.B.E., M.C.	August, 1953
Sir Eric Bowyer, K.C.B., K.B.E.	May, 1955

Reciprocal Agreements on Social Security

Reciprocal agreements on social security have been in force[1] with the countries listed below from the dates shown:

	Family Allowances	Industrial Injuries Insurance	National Insurance
Australia	January, 1954		January, 1954
Cyprus			January, 1957
Denmark[2]		May, 1954	
France		July, 1948	November, 1949 (July, 1948, for retirement pensions)
Guernsey	July, 1951		
Irish Republic		July, 1948[3]	July, 1948
Isle of Man	July, 1946	July, 1948	July, 1948
Israel		November, 1957	November, 1957
Italy		May, 1953	May, 1953
Jersey	July, 1954	August, 1954	August, 1954
Luxembourg		April, 1955	April, 1955
Malta		October, 1956	October, 1956
Netherlands		June, 1955	June, 1955
New Zealand	December, 1948		April, 1956
Northern Ireland	April, 1956	December, 1947	November, 1947
Norway[4]	February, 1958	February, 1958	February, 1958
Switzerland		June, 1954	June, 1954
Sweden[4]		June, 1957	June, 1957

[1] Agreements have also recently been signed with Belgium (May, 1957) and the Federal Republic of Germany (December, 1956) but await ratification before becoming fully operative. Agreements with Austria, Finland and Yugoslavia are being negotiated.

[2] A comprehensive agreement is being negotiated.

[3] Restricted to mariners.

[4] The agreement also covers the National Health Service.

INDEX

GEORGE ALLEN & UNWIN LTD
London: 40 Museum Street, W.C.1

Auckland: 24 Wyndham Street
Bombay: 15 Graham Road, Ballard Estate, Bombay 1
Calcutta: 17 Chittaranjan Avenue, Calcutta 13
Cape Town: 109 Long Street
Karachi: 254 Ingle Road
New Delhi: 13–14 Ajmeri Gate Extension, New Delhi 1
São Paulo: Avenida 9 de Julho 1138–Ap. 51
Sydney, N.S.W.: Bradbury House, 55 York Street
Toronto: 91 Wellington Street West

THE NEW WHITEHALL SERIES

is prepared under the auspices of the Royal Institute of Public Administration and is edited on its behalf by Sir Robert Fraser, O.B.E. The purpose of the series is to provide authoritative descriptions of the present work of the major Departments of the Central Government.

THE FOREIGN OFFICE
LORD STRANG

'If the efficiency of the Foreign Service is a more vital national interest than ever before, it is a duty for every serious citizen to read carefully this comprehensive and deeply informative book.'— *The Sunday Times.*

Demy 8vo, *3rd impression*, 18s. net

THE HOME OFFICE
SIR FRANK NEWSAM

'The book preserves a nice balance between official accuracy and human interest, and is written as if it were meant to be read.'—*The Times.*

Demy 8vo, *2nd impression*, 18s. net

THE COLONIAL OFFICE
SIR CHARLES JEFFRIES

No longer is the Colonial Office mainly concerned with supervising the working of the dependent governments. It is today the headquarters of an all-out effort to develop the resources of the overseas territories and to free them from obstacles to their progress and welfare. Sir Charles Jeffries shows how this development has come about and how the Colonial Office is equipped to meet the changing needs of the territories.

Demy 8vo, 18s. net

THE MINISTRY OF WORKS
SIR HAROLD EMMERSON
Demy 8vo, 15s. net

THE SCOTTISH OFFICE
SIR DAVID MILNE
Demy 8vo, 21s. net

GEORGE ALLEN AND UNWIN LTD